V

OUR LIVES

Voicing Our Stories/ Remaking Our Lives

Edited by

THE GRASSROOTS
WOMEN'S COLLECTIVE

SECOND STORY Press

Canadian Cataloguing in Publication Data

Voicing our stories/remaking our lives : women speak out

Includes bibliographical references.
ISBN 1-896764-25-8

1. Success. 2. Life change events — Psychological aspects.
3. Self-management (Psychology). 4.Women — Health and hygiene.
5. Women — Psychology. I. Grassroots Women's Collective.

HQ1206.V652 1999 158.1'082 C99-931766-0

Cover art by Laurie Lafrance
Edited by Beth McAuley and Jane Springer

Second Story Press gratefully acknowledges the assistance of the Ontario Arts Council and the Canada Council for the Arts for our publishing program. We acknowledge the financial support of the Government of Canada through the Book Publishing Industry Development Program.

Canada

Printed and bound in Canada

Published by
Second Story Press
720 Bathurst Street, Suite 301
Toronto, Ontario
M5S 2R4

To all women struggling against oppression:
to the past with its strengths,
to the present with its support from others,
and to the future
and the persistence
of our spirits.

Contents

Acknowledgements

We would like to thank the contributors for allowing us to publish their stories. They have received an honorarium for their work and any financial gain from the sale of this book is being donated to two designated women's services in our area.

We also wish to thank the following community members who so generously lent their time and energy to this project: Ilang Rivers and Ines Rios, St. Joseph's Immigrant Women's Centre; Jacqueline Roth, PATH Employment Services for the Disabled; Sharon Worchaluk, St. Matthew's House; Doreen Johnson, Sexual Assault Centre; Renate Manthei, Faye Halliday and Mo Fife, Hamilton Women's Centre; Rhonda Weston, Eva Googe, United Disabled Consumers and North End Information Services; Barbara Willis, Elizabeth Fry Society; Carolyn Wever and staff of Inasmuch House. Thanks also to Karen Williams who was with us at the start of the project; to Nairn Galvin, Women's Studies Programme, and to Rick Douglass-Chin, McMaster University; to Chris Sinding, Burlington Breast Cancer Survivor Network; to Maria Antelo, Spanish Counsellor, SISO; and Marlene Thomas.

We are grateful for the funding from the Social Sciences and Humanities Research Council of Canada and from Health Canada.

Thanks finally to our publishers and editors at Second Story Press, Beth McAuley and Lois Pike, for their work and commitment to the project.

Just a Journal Page

TRACY FRANKLIN

TODAY I BEGIN yet another journal. For the last year or two I have managed to keep writing pretty consistently. I'm glad, as writing is a good thing for me; it's therapeutic, I think. Let me begin with where I feel I am as of this moment.

1) My lover and I remain a little more topsy than turvy these days. I continue to realize that I must back off and leave him be, and just try and let things turn out how they may.

2) My daughters and I continue to form a stronger, healthier relationship. I'm learning to play!

3) I'm thriving in my life process. I know I can't change my past, but I feel hope in changing the present and future.

Perhaps, it sounds too solid for me, and in comparison with my earlier journals I must sound like either I'm lying or growing up a little bit. I don't know where I'm headed from here, but at least it has become clear that I'm moving forward. I know the hardest work is still ahead of me, though there is a major difference in what that means. All the work I've done so far has been for basic emotional/spiritual survival. Now I move forward towards acquiring a life. My life!

Introduction

THE GRASSROOTS WOMEN'S COLLECTIVE

Voicing Our Stories / Remaking Our Lives is a collection by women and about women. In these stories and poems, women speak about their lives from their points of view. These are not easy lives; the women tell of their struggles to overcome a wide range of trauma and violence.

Women's voices deserve to be heard; these are the voices of women who have been silenced in their homes and in their communities. The women are mothers, social workers, wives, activists. Their stories need to be told — stories about what they experienced and the work they undertook to become healthier women mentally, physically, emotionally, spiritually. Work doesn't mean only "paid work." Work also includes the personal work we do to become healthier people and the self-care that is required for us to live and survive.

Paid work is, of course, essential to our well-being and survival. In this collection, some women talk about how ill health has affected their work, or how bad working conditions have affected their health. But most talk about the work of becoming healthy women. Good health contributes to our self-esteem and self-respect, contributes to a more loving, nurturing and constructive home life. Our good health resonates in our workplaces — improves our interpersonal relationships, inspires us to pursue our personal goals and ambitions, helps us to provide better care for our children and helps us find respect on the job and in our daily lives.

The women writing in this collection are various: some are First Nations women, others have an Anglo-Saxon, Latin American, European or Middle Eastern heritage; some are immigrant, others non-immigrant; some live in urban communities, others in rural ones; some grew up on reserves; some write from prison. They tell stories of sexual abuse, harassment, alcoholism and mental breakdowns.

These women's narratives lend texture and richness to the harsh realities of life for many Canadian women. Consider, for example, the following statistics:

• In four out of five cases in Canada, the victims of spousal assault are women.

• In 1997, a total of 128 women were murdered in Canada; of those, 73 were killed by an intimate partner. (Ministry of Women's Equality, "Efforts Must Continue to End Violence Against Women, Hammell Says." Press release, October 28, 1998.)

• In the case of spousal killings, police officers were aware of previous domestic violence between the victim and the suspect in over half of the cases (56 percent). (Statistics Canada, *The Daily*, Thursday, 28 May 1998.)

• In 1996, children under 18 were victims in 22 percent of all violent crimes reported to police. In family-related assaults, fathers were responsible for 73 percent of physical assaults and 98 percent of sexual assaults. (Statistics Canada, *The Daily*, Thursday, 28 May 1998.)

• In 1995, women in Ontario earned on average fifty-seven

cents to every dollar earned by a man. (Federal-Provincial/ Territorial Ministers Responsible for the Status of Women, *Economic Gender Equality Indicators.* Government of Canada, 1997.)

• Single mothers with children run the greatest risk of poverty among all economic groups in Canada; 56.8 percent of all poor families were headed by single mothers in 1995. The poverty rate for children in families headed by a single mother was 61.9 percent, nearly five times that of children in two-parent families (14.1 percent). The average income for a poor female single-parent family was $14,612. About 42 percent of female single-parent families relied on social assistance in 1994, compared with about 8 percent of two-parent families. (Christa Freiler, *Benefiting Canada's Children: Perspectives on Gender and Social Responsibility.* Government of Canada, 1998.)

• A recent Government of Canada report observed the ambivalence with which our government treats women, expecting single mothers to both stay at home with their children and be economically independent simultaneously. Such a contradictory message was demonstrated by the Ontario government's criticism of women for failing to be at home to prepare hot breakfasts for their children, while, at the same time, introducing policies that required women to work for their welfare benefits when their youngest child reached the age of three. (Christa Freiler, *Benefiting Canada's Children: Perspectives on Gender and Social Responsibility.* Government of Canada, 1998.)

• In an international ranking of countries and child benefits in 1994, Canada (real GDP/Capita $20,950) ranked second only to the United States (real GDP/Capita $24,680) in terms of comparative national wealth and placed last in its allotment of basic child benefits ($936 basic child benefit, as opposed to Austria's first-ranking $3,920). (Christa Freiler, *Benefiting Canada's Children: Perspectives on Gender and Social Responsibility*. Government of Canada, 1998.)

• In 1993, 28 percent of visible minority women and 33 percent of Native women lived in a low-income situation. (Status of Women Canada, "Statistics on Women in Canada," 1998.)

• In 1996, one-third of all Native children under fifteen lived in a single-parent family, twice the rate of the general population. In urban areas, the rate was 46 percent. (Statistics Canada, *The Daily*, Tuesday, January 13, 1998.)

The women in *Voicing Our Stories / Remaking Our Lives* represent a mere "drop in the bucket" of women who endure and who have survived some form of violence, whether it be physical, sexual or economic.

GATHERING THE STORIES

In 1994, the community research co-ordinator of the McMaster Research Centre for the Promotion of Women's Health invited a group of community representatives to a meeting. The Centre, sponsored by the Social Sciences and Humanities Research Council and the National Health Research and Development Program of Canada, has been committed to developing new community-based strategies that promote health. The representatives were from women's groups, agencies and workplaces in the area. A series of meetings were held to discuss the research needs of the women in the community and to decide on possible research projects on women, work and health. Community representatives complained that community groups were tired of being "researched" by academics and proposed a collection of women's stories about their experiences of work and health. We formed the Grassroots Women's Collective, an advisory committee which would oversee the project. As a committee, we wanted the project to focus on women's experiences rather than on existing research. We wanted to hear from women at a grassroots level and intentionally avoided developing a project based on traditional research, analysis and evaluations. Our aim was to document women's lives and struggles by eliciting their stories. By doing so, we felt we could offer women a chance to have their voices heard.

We believe that women's stories should be written down so that people can hear what women are suffering and what they are doing to fight against discrimination. We wanted to celebrate and document work that has been done already by women trying to work and to organize. We wanted to give people a voice, allow them to tell their stories, help them realize that their stories are important enough to be published and to bring to the public eye what does happen. We wanted to offer tangible, candid, concrete accounts of women's lives.

At the outset, we were not particularly looking for stories of childhood or past trauma. Yet we chose the working title "Telling Our Stories" because it suggested that women, in telling their stories and talking about their experiences, needed to articulate more than just a specific link between their (paid) work and their health. They could include whatever they felt was necessary to complete the picture of what health and work meant to them. The title also suggested a tradition of talking amongst women. The very form of narrative readily lent itself to that articulation: women would allow their voices to flow with a multiplicity of focal points, rather than only one.

To start the outreach, we mailed a flyer and letter together to some 120 women's groups and agencies throughout the region asking for women's stories. We described ourselves as a group of local community activists from a variety of workplaces who had come together to work on the "Telling Our Stories" project. The project aimed to publish a collection of women's first-hand accounts of their health problems caused by work — related to difficulties such as discrimination, violence, poverty, unemployment or unhealthy workplaces — and of their collective struggle for social change. We understood women's work to be work done in the home, or at an outside workplace, paid or unpaid, and including women's caregiving for elders and children. We understood women's health to be not only physical but also emotional and spiritual well-being. We emphasized that the project would encourage women who had been marginalized by various oppressions to voice their experiences and by doing so, participate in creating knowledge about women's realities and lives. Such a woman-centred creation of knowledge would contribute to future work with women; it would be one way to replace "research *about* women" by providing research that comes directly *from* the women themselves.

We followed up our initial mail-out with phone calls and presentations made at agencies or women's groups' meetings. Specific contacts were made with potential contributors by the Grassroots Women's Collective. Blank tapes and exercise books were left with one community centre. We had translations of the flyer made in Spanish, Taga-payo (Filipino), French, Vietnamese and Portuguese. Many women sent us their stories on their own initiative. However, we also offered to tape, transcribe or translate stories for women who did not want to write them or who wrote in a language other than English. Some stories were offered orally, and these were recorded, transcribed and edited with the author's feedback; two stories were translated. The whole process took five years: to gather the stories, select them and publish them. Some of the writers have chosen to publish under a pseudonym. We chose these stories because they convey vividly the struggles to achieve and maintain health, and they do so with honesty. They provide a spectrum of experiences and strategies for healing.

THE WOMEN'S VOICES

What comes across in *Voicing Our Stories / Remaking Our Lives* is the incredible strength women have. Their stories are about surviving, changing and sometimes triumphing, and offer hope for others who are living through similar experiences.

There are many themes that arise from listening to these women's stories about seeking and making better lives for themselves. One is the use of journals or writing in women's healing. Tracy Franklin offers us a journal page as a way of demonstrating the power that journals have as "archaeological" sources of the past and the present — to document women's lives, women's voices. For some of the women, the telling and writing of their stories is a very painful but healing process. They have spoken of how it taps into their emotional history and how this cannot be done lightly. Often they need to step back from the process or risk being overwhelmed. Still, the telling is part of the recovery and working through of the pain, the claiming of a new identity based on surviving, enduring and even triumphing. In speaking about the internal suffering and the past events, they can come to some understanding of the external causes and move away from self-blame and self-hatred. Even in the most difficult stories in this collection, there is always the narrative voice of someone who has seen it through to the other end, someone who has been able to get so far beyond the hurt that they can write about it. They are writing about a past that they have struggled to overcome.

For the most part, these women look forward to the book's publication because it will help them feel that they are "not so alone." Women so often go through their struggles alone and are isolated from one another. This book may offer a thread to the community of women who have struggled and who continue to struggle in their lives.

Many of the stories speak about the work of mothering. Terry Weir identifies as a mother and asks why mothering is so undervalued in our society. Toni Sano writes about the challenges of mothering four special-needs children, while overcoming her own clinical depression; Alexandra describes how the responsibilities of being a single mother on social assistance brought to her life a stability and a desire to succeed, which she had never experienced as a depressed and suicidal adolescent fleeing a dysfunctional home. Carol Henhawk relates the way in which physical and sexual abuse, family substance abuse and frequent dislocations both on the reserve and in the city, resulted in her own struggles with alcohol, suicidal behaviour and abusive relationships. It was the birth of a daughter that changed her life: "I was going to be there for her. I was going to change things and I did." Henhawk has since worked in a shelter for abused Native women and with adolescents.

Many of the women speak of the responsibility of children and often how isolated and without support mothers are. They speak of the amount of labour there is in household work and management as well as in nurturing children. They speak of ways in which they have tried to balance this work and their own educational goals. Kathleen Moore demonstrates the resourcefulness of women as she learns to raise her children and maintain and repair her own home alone, in the perpetual absence of her sailor husband. She also learns the meaning of self-acceptance as she comes to embrace her own identity. In her healing journey, Margaret Thomas describes her determination to establish her financial and personal independence before marrying and raising a family. Through intense inner work and a powerful sense of her own Native spirituality, she has come to terms with the painful traumas of her childhood.

Most of the women speak of the importance of finding rewarding employment, not just for the money — although that is often crucial — but also for the sense of fulfillment and accomplishment paid labour offers. Henhawk and Thomas speak of the value they feel in being able to help others who are going through some of the problems that they have experienced. On the other hand, Marie Sanson writes about the risk women take in the workforce. Because of others' expectations, women risk damaging their personal relationships; they also risk sexual harassment on the job. Yet women can achieve great things despite these and other barriers.

A number of these stories speak of child sexual abuse, wife battering and family violence. We can see in these stories the immediate and long-term effects of this violence. There are physical and mental repercussions: eating disorders, self-mutilation, alcoholism, depression, suicidal attempts.

Yet the stories return to the resourcefulness of women. Women take control of the home front; find work to support themselves and their children; learn to say no to dangerous situations; learn self-respect; hold on to dreams and ambitions; find the way out of the trauma, out of the abyss. Again and again, the women return to the importance of achieving personal and life goals, which may include their education, work or spirituality. They document how hard it is to achieve these goals but they offer ways of struggling to keep trying.

LOOKING FORWARD

The words in *Voicing Our Stories / Remaking Our Lives* evoke tales that have been concealed by women because the stories have been taboo, forbidden, unacceptable. The women are honest and direct; they write from their experiences. While some women have come through their difficulties, others are still struggling. Yet all of the women here have given voice to issues that many others experience and still struggle to overcome.

We hope that these narratives will inspire women who are trying to continue their personal work. We hope too that the stories will help those in the health professions — therapists, shelter workers, social workers — to better respect and understand women who have endured abuse, harassment, racism or poverty. We hope these stories inspire health professionals to offer women improved and more appropriate services, and develop a deeper appreciation of what kinds of supports women and children need. For example D. Lussier Nanson shows us that perceptive and sensitive measures continually need to be in place both to detect and to prevent the abuse of young children. In their stories of immigrant women, Elvira Herrera and Mona Aziz demonstrate the need for service providers to be culturally sensitive. Service providers should be aware not only of the challenges of adjustment facing immigrant women, but also of the possible addiction struggles or physical and sexual abuse issues with which they may also be grappling. Bernadette Alpen poses disturbing questions concerning power, sensitivity and trust in relationships between child abuse intervention service providers and client-families.

Many of the stories in this collection demonstrate that help is not always available to children or adult women. As readers, we need to ask ourselves why this is. In Ontario today, a crisis exists in health and social services for women. Over the last four years, fiscal conservative measures in the province have eliminatd many key services for women and children and continue to threaten existing gains. Take for example, hospital closures; a freeze on public housing for the homeless and for abused women and their children; a 21.6 percent cut to welfare benefits; drastic cuts to education, daycare and to services for female minorities and women's shelters; removal of rent restrictions; and the overturning of pay equity laws. *Voicing Our Stories / Remaking Our Lives* demonstrates how women use their own resources to find their way. Sometimes — and especially in times such as these — it is only by chance that women find support and direction from "official" services. How can this situation be overcome or improved?

Voicing Our Stories / Remaking Our Lives will reach beyond women in struggle and the professionals who provide support to them; the stories will reach friends and other family members. The women's narratives clearly demonstrate the need for all of us to advocate for safe families, safe childhoods, constructive and nurturing parenting and the right to be respected in the workplace. By drawing on women's knowledge, we can better develop programs that promote health and well-being, that more effectively train service providers and teach strategies for community health. Speaking out and voicing one's story is a strategy. It is a process that contributes to women's recovery: for the women themselves, for women who read their stories and for professionals who help women and children.

— *The Grassroots Women's Collective*
Mary O'Connor
Marcela Leighton Krautter
Maggie Fischbuch
Reva Bomberry
Mona Aziz

I Didn't Marry a Sailor

KATHLEEN MOORE

I know I'm not the only woman in this leaky boat: I'm married to a sailor. These situations will be familiar to some of you. You need only insert long-distance trucker, airline pilot, deep sea diver, geologist, pipe liner, offshore oil rigger, fisherman.

It is approaching Christmas Eve, and once again I am wondering if I will be spending the holiday with my husband. He has taken a last-minute tow upbound through the Welland Canal just before it closes. I have been assured that every effort will be made to get him home for Christmas.

Don't get me wrong, he works for a great group of people and we are well provided for. The employee and dependent benefit package alone are beyond the reach of most people. In case of emergency or family crisis, I've been told I need only call the head office and they will have my husband headed for home on the first available means of transportation. I haven't found the crisis yet that would compel me to make that call.

I am married to a sailor, but I didn't marry a sailor. My mother married a sailor and so did my grandmother. We were married six years before my husband returned to the work he had fallen in love with as a boy. He rushed home one day to tell me there was a tug in the St. Lawrence that needed a wheelsman, and he had been offered the job. He had his discharge book in hand and his ditty bag over his shoulder in less time than it took me to change the baby's diaper and quiet the six-year-old. Hell, I didn't even know he owned a discharge book and ditty bag. I didn't know it then, but that day set the pattern we would follow for the next eighteen years. He had one foot out the door before it occurred to him to ask how I felt about the situation. His last words were, "Well, you didn't say I couldn't go!"

That first trip away was an adventure for both of us. I busied myself redecorating the living room. He rediscovered sailing, his first love. We've all had one. The kind that wakes you in the middle of the night with longing and regret for things undone. I've been told since, by those much wiser than myself, that it is in the nature of some people to climb mountains because they are there, and battle those elements of nature that cannot be beaten. It's as if something calls to them and they have to answer. If this is true, it's a fact I find difficult to accept.

I'm a nester, always have been, and I come from a long line of them, but I must admit they were all women. When he left on that first trip, I could have said no. I could have said choose. I could have said don't come back. I should have said go to hell. For a long time I blamed myself for giving in; after all, I should have been more assertive. I come from a long line of strong women. Did I disappoint them by wimping out? Did I let them down?

I did exactly what they had done before me. I tried to give my children an environment to grow in and hold together what was left of my family. My mother worked everyday in a factory to provide for her two children. She chose forty-four hours a week in a sweatshop over a bad marriage to a sailor.

My grandmother had the choosing done for her. Divorce wasn't an option in her day. Grandpa was serving his country as a Chief Petty Officer in the Royal Canadian Navy. His time at home was sporadic and short until the late Forties when he retired from the Navy and took a job on shore as a machinist. Great-grandma started raising her family in a sod hut on a quarter section of the Prairies while Great-grandpa was off working on the railway project of the century.

Somewhere in the vast gene pool I inherited was the resourcefulness I needed. My husband's attitude seemed to be, "You'll manage, what can be so tough about taking care of two kids, a big black dog and an old rented house?" Besides, wouldn't I feel better knowing where he was nights and knowing how happy he was? What a crock of shit! But for a marriage that had reached the rocky point, it seemed to be the answer at the time. We had lost the passion in our relationship, but didn't yet have the maturity to form a friendship. This solution seemed less traumatic than a divorce. I guess what we were saying was that we didn't really want to live together, but didn't have the guts to throw in the towel. So he sailed.

Surprisingly enough, considering my background, I had acquired the notion that a wife should be a personal asset to her husband: guard his material assets, raise his children diligently, uphold his moral values and be a credit to him socially. None of the female ancestors had left notes on what was expected of a man, other than providing food and lodging for his family. I guess they didn't get much from their men, and really didn't expect much from them, or from life in general.

When my husband finished his first season on the tugs, he decided it was time we purchased a house. After all, he was a man of means, he had two bank accounts and a reliable income. He chose a house in the neighbourhood I had grown up in, down by the waterfront where we could hear the boat whistles. It was an old house with a huge back yard. Old houses are hardly maintenance-free, but over the years we have managed to alter or renovate and upgrade most of the troublesome features of our two-and-a-half-storey brick dwelling. It was decided early on that I would be the one to deal with contractors, builders and repairmen. With my husband home on a hit-or-miss basis, the continuity of a contracted repair would be lost if it depended on him being there. If I ever reach the pearly gates, St. Peter is probably going to say: "Well, I really would rather talk to your husband." I'd be willing to send him on ahead, but he would probably botch the job, with the excuse that his wife usually handles these things.

Take the back yard for example, I think he has mowed it twice in seventeen years. I asked him to help weed the flower beds one spring. We each took a side of the 33-metre yard and I was grateful for the help. I was only about half done my side when he asked what else I needed help with. A little bell should have gone off in my head, but being somewhat of an optimist I just thought it was great to have him home and willing to help around the yard. He had literally pulled up everything in the bed. Weeds, perennials, biannuals and all. I still think he did it deliberately. When asked, he now says, "The yard? I let my wife take care of that; she knows about flowers and things." I will admit though, he is the darndest hole digger I've ever seen. You just have to direct him to the correct spot, keep an eye on him and tell him when to stop.

It has been difficult to deal with contractors and repairmen. They would all rather talk to my husband. I'm so tired of mechanics and servicemen in general who think that if you're wearing a skirt, you've got no balls and don't know squat about anything. If a repairman comes to my house to fix my dryer, the one that I have used for at least eighteen years, and asks my husband (if he is home) what the problem is, brother is he in trouble.

Auto mechanics are particularly troublesome with their preconceived notion that women are not mechanically inclined. When I was growing up, all the other kids on the block were boys. I hardly knew what a dress was until my tenth birthday, when my mother declared that it was time I started acting like a lady and quit running around the bayfront. By the time I was a teenager, I was building model cars and airplanes or had my head stuck under the hood of one of the boy's cars. Even so, I should have a nickel for every time a mechanic has told me to have my husband bring the car back when he gets off work. Yeah, sure buddy, you want to wait until December? My husband might drive the car once a year, I drive it every day and I know when a wheel bearing is shot. I have finally found a garage where they don't try to look behind me to find my husband every time I pull in. Over the years they have actually learned to trust my limited knowledge. But there was still that awful moment when my husband would say, "Hell, I could have got that done cheaper by Joe down the street."

My husband isn't a handy person, so over the years we have acquired an assortment of reference material on making home repairs. I often scan this material as a change of pace from my usual reading. I expect to have to change an occasional washer in a tap and want to be prepared. I find dripping taps intolerable and know I wouldn't be able to leave something like that untended until my husband makes one of his appearances. And sometimes there are bigger jobs I can't leave unattended. For example, one night there was a terrible crash in the bathroom and then both children started hollering, "I didn't do it." The old wall-mounted sink had finally given way and crashed to the floor, breaking the pipes in the process. It was a Sunday night. Where would I find a repairman at that hour that wouldn't cost an arm and a leg? First order of business was to shut off the water at the main, because we hadn't renovated the bathroom and didn't have individual shut-offs for the water supply. The next day was a school day, the kids would need water in the morning. What to do? I wanted to panic and run to the nearest man (grandfather, father, repairman). Where the hell was my husband? Weren't these the occasions when husbands proved their worth, patted the little woman on the head and told her not to worry, he could fix it in a jiffy?

Once the water was shut off, things didn't seem quite so bad. I sat down at the top of the stairs in the puddle of water coming from the bathroom, took a couple of deep breaths and mustered those resourceful genes I knew I had. I had watched pipe being soldered a dozen times. I knew what was needed. Calm the kids, get them busy with every towel in the house and make a temporary retreat to the basement to look over the supplies on hand. I dove into my husband's spare-parts bins. Praise the Lord, pipe caps! When my husband makes a repair to the house, he saves every scrap of material left over. Thank goodness for his thrift.

It took a few minutes to assemble the necessary equipment: pipe cutter, butane torch, solder, emery cloth, flux paste. I could do this, I really could! I had one little problem. I had never applied sparker to torch and was scared to death. What if I blew the house up? I went back up to the bathroom and tried not to think about it as I cut the old pipes below the damage, cleaned them with the emery cloth and applied the flux paste. I sat there in the puddle of water for a few moments trying to breathe slowly and muster my courage to light the torch. I did it, and the little bathroom was soon filled with the acrid smell of melting flux paste and solder. Once I conquered my fear of the torch I became determined that not only could I do this job, I could do it well. When the solder had cooled I went to the basement and opened the main. Then I ran like hell upstairs. Son of a gun, my little soldering job held. The pipe caps were secure, there were no leaks. The kids were amazed; Mom had saved the day.

There were other kinds of trials and tribulations that didn't always turn out so well, though. After a few years of sailing my husband was sent on longer and longer jobs. Sometimes he didn't make it directly back home, but if he got close enough, a three-hour drive or less, the kids and I would jump into the old car and take a chance on catching him in port. We were usually pretty lucky, but the farewells were murder. The kids would cry most of the way back home and I would usually end up joining them, while telling them there was nothing to cry about, Daddy would be home soon. When we got home, the kids would run out to play, distracted by friends. I found my own distraction in the occasional drink. The occasions became more frequent. I didn't drink until the kids were safely asleep, but soon it took longer and longer to reach the point where I didn't hurt anymore. Life as I knew it had reached an all-time low. I had married young, married the wrong man. I still loved him, somehow, but he kept running away from me on his bloody boats. If he had had a passionate fixation on another woman, I could have done something about it, but a boat, how do you fight that?

When I didn't have a hangover, I had a migraine. A bad one could last two or three days. The doctor prescribed pain killers for the migraines. It didn't take me long to OD and end up in the hospital. They say a person who attempts suicide is crying out for help. They're right, but what they don't tell you is that you feel like a complete idiot when you wake up and find you have failed. Now you are faced with the prospect of justifying yourself to complete strangers. You probably did this to yourself because you were without an emotional outlet in your own circle and now they want you to open up to someone you've never met before. Not to mention that this stranger would rather be helping the maimed and diseased who are suffering from non-self-inflicted wounds. The only one who can really help you is yourself. Yet after years of being on my own, I was still pretending I had a husband. I was still trying to please him, consult him when possible, bow to his wishes. The day I came home from the hospital, I didn't want to return to my old life. My husband told the doctor he had no idea why I would do such a thing, it must have been accidental. He was half right, he really didn't have any idea about what was going on in my life.

I gave up drinking. I had started to investigate, on my own, the causes of my migraine headaches. Along the way I read about alcoholism. We all know now that alcohol is a depressant and can only lead to a tightening downward spiral. Even without the alcohol, my depression deepened. I found myself crying at odd times and then I would get insomnia. The doctor prescribed antidepressants. I became a zombie. I was no longer crying, but I was unable to laugh and eventually unable to function normally. I felt like I was running in oatmeal. My arms and legs no longer had the strength to get me across a room or up a flight of stairs. In a fog, I phoned my pharmacist about the medication I was taking, and without consulting my doctor, gradually weaned myself off it. I continued my investigation into the causes of migraines and started keeping a daily log of substances I consumed. It's been ten years now since I've had a migraine. For a long time I wouldn't take so much as an aspirin.

I decided that I would never again allow another human being to dictate my life and drive me to the point of desperation. As another tactic of self-preservation, I took my own bedroom. I moved the children into a room together and took the empty room for myself. My room. My haven. It was a start. I started saying, No. My life will be what I make of it. My husband is the transient, not me.

I had been going through life on everyone else's coattails. I was my mother's child, my husband's wife, my children's mother. Who the hell was I, anyway? I changed doctors and found one that didn't have a prescription for everything. I found a counsellor I could have faith in and could trust. I started to take a more passive rather than an active interest in my husband's whereabouts. I stopped chasing him all over the waterways. I would be here when he could get home, but he would have to come to me. When his vessel was in port, and I was invited aboard, my interest re-activated itself and I spent time learning what I could about his work. I realized that my relationship with my husband would have to be based on what he was most familiar with, his work, and it would be up to me to build the other part of my life, the part without him. I became active in my community. I volunteered at the nearby school, coached the swim team and assisted in teaching non-swimmers how to get their faces wet without experiencing a full-blown panic. When our youngest child entered high school, I went back to school. I could do anything if I wanted to badly enough. I became a force to be reckoned with. I still go to school, college level now, and probably always will. I have found I enjoy stretching and using my mind for something other than balancing the chequebook or finding another way to cook hamburger.

For years my biggest fear was that I would make a mistake, choose the wrong item or colour or — heaven forbid — not get the best bargain. You can't live life without making a mistake unless you stand perfectly still and do absolutely nothing, but even then you will probably pick the wrong place to stand and will get stepped on.

Through trial and error I have learned how to lay a tile floor (the kids call me "Queen of the Tile"), install a washing machine and replace a fan motor on a refrigerator. The biggest thing I have learned is that it is okay to try and fail. The world won't dissolve beneath your feet, and having failed, you can always try again.

It's okay to say my marriage isn't perfect. Whose is? Is an absentee husband any worse than an absentee landlord? I like my husband now. We've been through a lot, some of it together. It is coming up twenty-four years for us now. I think I'll keep him. We're becoming best buddies. I have him because I finally let him go.

Both my children are girls, and I know from talking to them that they have gone through some rough times, too. I've always tried to be honest and upfront with my daughters about anything they wanted to discuss. I could never talk to my mother, she was too busy keeping food on the table. Their dad wasn't always there for them when he should have been, and sometimes when he could have been. I have had to be both father and mother to my girls, and as hard as I have tried, I'm not their father and can never totally fill their need for him. For a long time I tried to be the catalyst that kept his relationship with the children ticking, but that is a job I have learned to stay away from. If my husband expects to have a relationship with his children it is up to him to maintain it, take the bruises when he fails and reap the rewards when he is successful. They all seem much better for it.

It hasn't always been easy. I've fallen on my face more than once. I have found that the more I gave, the more was expected of me. Most of the time it was easier to go the extra mile than it was to protest. I've run myself to the end of my rope a few times. The realization of how far I had gone in picking up the slack of an absentee husband became clear to me the day I was up on the roof of our two-and-a-half-storey house cleaning the gutters. My neighbour from across the street came running over, begging me not to jump. I held up the hose to indicate that I was just cleaning the gutters and started laughing so hard I almost did fall off.

My new relationship with my life happened over the years, gradually. I was still my children's mother, my husband's wife, but as the children grew and became independent I found I was having trouble identifying myself. I had avoided the problem by keeping busy. My life had been spent fulfilling the needs of others, often before they realized the need themselves. I felt that I was letting them down if I made demands in return. As their need for me lessened, I became a non-entity, unwilling to demand my rightful place, avoiding a disturbance at all costs. To find myself, I had to find the strength and will to defeat alcohol and fight depression. Now I work at keeping myself well.

Depression has reared its ugly head again recently, but I've travelled this road before and now I'm prepared. With the help of my counsellor, I'm learning to voice my opinions, I'm claiming my place and recognizing my right to be happy. I have the right to feel good about myself, to feel worthwhile; I've earned it.

You can't expect someone to learn from your mistakes and experiences if you're not willing to delve into your own feelings fully. I think that was the hardest lesson to learn, being honest with myself. I'm not afraid anymore to tell my daughters "I don't know, but let's find out together," or that I made a mistake they may want to try to avoid making. It is no guarantee, but they stand a hell of a lot better chance if I tell them honestly why I made the decision that grew into a mistake.

My oldest daughter has settled into a happy relationship with a man she can share her life with. He's a good provider and he's home every night, and with their two sons they make a solid family. They've had their setbacks, but have worked through them together. I have the pleasure of watching my grandchildren grow with two parents who are there on a daily basis to help them.

My youngest daughter starts university next year. She has been working part-time since she was eleven years old and is a wise hand with a dollar. She buys her own clothes and has saved enough money to travel to the East and West Coasts of Canada as well as to Florida. We have always talked openly. She's not sure about the changes she sees in me. We talk even more now. She is making plans for her productive years, looking forward to finding a partner. She loves her father, and I would never want to take that away from her, but the life I've lived is not the life for her. Perhaps I've managed to teach her more than I could have dreamed possible.

Changes

TRACY FRANKLIN

There's a time when everything begins to change
Looking around, you find nothing familiar
just strange
Things aren't the way they used to be
and the road ahead becomes difficult to see

You wonder if things will ever be the same
there's at least familiarity in precious pain
This is reality and no longer a game
How you wish you could grab onto the past
taking your time, afraid of moving too fast

Finally it's time to carry on
A lot of what hurts inside will soon be gone
You take the steps needed once and for all
Knowing it's time to tear down your wall

Make no promises
Let your eyes see
what really
matters

After All, Everyone Has a Mother

TERRY WEIR

Being a homemaker and a mother is at times a very stressful and emotionally draining job. It is one that receives no vacations or weekends off and the typical workday is twelve to sixteen hours. A homemaker and mother doesn't come home from work to a lovely meal, a clean house and fresh laundry. Her day usually ends when she's taken care of the needs of everyone else, sometimes neglecting her own, and finally goes to bed. Then, she is often asked why she is so tired when all she does is sit around all day and watch soap operas!

I am a thirty-one-year-old mother of three and have worked outside the home as well as being a homemaker. At times being at home with the children is stressful and even frightening. Think about what we are responsible for: here are little people who put all their trust in our hands, their lives depend on us, and the person they become is in large part because of what we teach them. Yet we receive no preparation or training for this; we have no one to tell us how to deal with our fears and the stress of this responsibility or its effects on our bodies. Depression, fatigue, migraines, headaches, deep sadness and feelings of worthlessness are just some of the symptoms that women experience. Sometimes we feel that in the process of taking care of others we lose ourselves — we discover that we have no identity outside our home. We are mothers, wives, but rarely do we find the time to just be women.

I have gone through times of extreme depression, sadness and fatigue with nowhere to turn to for help. There are too few organizations to help women. The few that do exist are usually under-advertised and under-funded so they are not accessible to all who require them.

Women are the founders of life and we should be appreciated and accommodated. A paid job is no more important than that of the homemaker and mother. We mould the people of our future. What job could possibly be more important than developing the personalities and characters of our future leaders, politicians, doctors and other workers? Yet, in spite of the great importance of this task, we receive little or no recognition, we do not get paid except for self-gratification, and we get no benefits.

I've learned through experience that we homemakers and mothers need to take time out to care for ourselves, because we are as important in this world as any and everyone else. After all, everyone has a mother.

My Problems with Alcohol

ELVIRA HERRERA

This story is about the problems and difficulties I have faced both in my home and at work because of my illness, that is, alcoholism. My history of alcoholism began when I married for the second time. I married for the first time when I was fourteen years old, in 1964. My first husband used to drink, but he was not an alcoholic. I left him because he was aggressive and often used violence against me. I had five children with him, four boys and a girl, who died when she was sixteen months old. Two of the children grew up with me and the other two with their father's family.

My second marriage took place in 1974. My second husband was an alcoholic, although he never admitted it. When I met him, three years before we married, I always saw him drinking, but I never thought that it was going to affect my life. But it did. My husband would drink almost every day and would spend two weeks drinking without stopping. Then he would stop drinking and start vomiting and I had to clean it all up. The smell was unbearable. It was then that I began to drink, so I wouldn't smell the stench. Everything was all right at the beginning, when I would drink only for a day, but then my drinking increased. By that time, our daughter had been born.

I did not drink during the pregnancy, but after the birth my alcoholism increased and I began to have difficulties, for I was drinking up to three days in a row.

My husband's reaction when he saw that I was drinking so much was terrible, sometimes he used to beat me up, then my children would intervene and it was an insufferable problem. When I was well, I was aware of everything I was doing and I would swear that I would never drink again. But in the end I knew that it was a lie, and my drinking went on and on. Three years after my alcoholism began, I still did not feel that my health was damaged. However, soon after that I had to emigrate to Honduras because of the war that was going on in my country, Nicaragua. I left with my daughter, leaving my four other children behind with my second husband.

As soon as I arrived in Honduras, I started to work as a seamstress. I did not have a fixed place to work, like a factory or even my own home, so I went to people's houses when they requested my services. I had some money with me and my husband was going to join me after my arrival because, since he was a military man, he could not leave Nicaragua with me. But he never came, and about two months later, I heard the news that he had disappeared. I felt lonely and helpless, and I started drinking again. I missed work for two days and gave the excuse that my daughter was sick, so I did not lose the job. But I started drinking more frequently, up to the point where I did lose my job.

Almost two years after being a refugee in Honduras, my daughter and I went back to Nicaragua with the few things I had. But even in my country it was not easy. My sons were there, but they could not help me because they hardly made enough money for themselves. The two that I had raised were working for the government. By this time my daughter was already six years old and I registered her in a public school. I began looking for work and found a job with a woman who owned a sewing factory. That went well for a while, but difficulties began when I started drinking heavily again. Well, the owner of the factory had the same problem. She also drank a lot and so did two of my co-workers, and every Saturday we would drink together. Ah! when I was drunk I used to say that my husband was an army colonel, and who knows what else I said, but it reached the ears of the government. I began to get threats that my daughter was going to be kidnapped, as a way to lure back my husband, and if he appeared, they would put him in jail.

I had to leave Nicaragua again. My daughter and I left on December 22nd and travelled to Costa Rica, another neighbouring country. I was looking for a cousin who lived there and who had money. I had no luck. She was out of the country and I only had her telephone number and not her address, and just money to live on for a couple of days. Not knowing anybody there and feeling so desperate, the desire to drink started up again, but I restrained myself because I knew that my daughter needed me very much. December 24th arrived and by then I did not have a penny, not even to pay for lodgings or food. Every day I would dial my cousin's telephone number without getting an answer. When she saw my situation, the owner of the boarding house where I was staying offered me room and board in exchange for my help with hotel jobs. I immediately accepted, since I had already been looking for work in several places but with no results, because everywhere they asked me for letters of reference and I did not know anyone in Costa Rica. And so I spent December 24th without money and without being able to give my daughter at least one little gift for Christmas.

The two of us spent that evening alone, locked in the little room in the basement that the owner had given me in exchange for work. I remember that I cried all night because I felt like the unhappiest woman in the world. In the New Year, after I had already been working in the boarding house for fifteen days, I phoned my cousin (I phoned her every day) and I got an answer. It was my niece. I explained my problem to her and she sent a person to pick me up. My cousin came back three days later. My cousin told me that she was going to help me, but what she actually did was exploit me. She made me do all the housework by myself. I felt humiliated and drank every night. It got worse, and when she realized what was happening, she threatened to take away my daughter and send her to a convent, so I decided to leave her house as soon as possible.

I found a room for my daughter and me to live in. It was a small and dirty room, but what else could I do? I began to look for work again. I was desperate for money. It reached the point where I had to ask for food for my little daughter. I went into a small restaurant and asked the woman who was sitting in front of the bar whether she could give me a bit of food for my daughter, because she had not even had breakfast. The woman, her name was Patricia, went to the kitchen and brought me some food. A little later an elderly woman came out, she was Patricia's mother and the owner of the restaurant. Her name was Nena. She asked what was happening to me, and I told her that I did not have a job and that I was desperate. Nena offered me work at that very moment and hired me as a cook in her restaurant. I thanked God for having brought her to me and promised never to drink again. But, deep down inside, I knew that was a lie, that at the first opportunity I would drink again, and so it was. I started drinking again, but Nena was so good and did not fire me. On the contrary, she became fond of my daughter, who ate at the restaurant every day and went to the same school as all of Nena's grandchildren. This was how my great friendship with her began.

But of course my alcoholism was increasing day by day, up to the point where Nena took care of my daughter while I was sick. But I always kept on working. Nena noticed that I could sew very well and gave me a sewing machine so that I could work in my small room and not have to work at the restaurant every day. She also rented a small and very affordable house for me and my daughter, and I began to work at home as a seamstress. I was able to build up a pretty nice business. But, as usual, my problem continued. I could go for a few days without drinking. Many times, however, when I began to think about the children I left behind in Nicaragua, I would feel terribly depressed and would turn to alcohol for consolation. I could not meet my commitments to my clients. However, I never let myself down. I carried on and always worked hard to catch up when I stopped drinking. Every day, though, I felt the illness deteriorating my body.

Three years went by. The war in Nicaragua was still going on. My daughter and I knew that we could not go back to our country. My husband, who had been reported missing, was a sympathizer of the old Somosa government and the new communist regime was sending to prison anybody who was associated with Somosa. I thought of the possibility of emigrating to Canada. A niece had gone to Canada a few years before and wrote me a letter when I was in Costa Rica. In her letter, she told me of the wonderful educational opportunities that Canada could offer to my daughter, who was then twelve years old. Since I wanted the best for her, I took the chance and left Costa Rica. We joined another group of thirteen people from Central America who also wanted to emigrate to Canada. We took a Pan Am flight from San José to Montreal. My niece — who was then living in Toronto — was going to meet us in Montreal. The problem was that our group was held in Miami because we had no visas for Canada or the United States. From Miami, we were shipped to New York where, without a single explanation, immigration officials ordered five of us to board a plane for Hamilton, Ontario. The rest of the group stayed in New York. Finally, we arrived in Hamilton in April 1988. When immigration officers went aboard the plane to ask about our purposes for coming to Canada, we all replied: "We are refugees." The officers asked many questions and, since none of us knew a soul in Hamilton, they sent us to a downtown hotel where newcomers used to lodge. The next day we were taken to St. Joseph's convent where we lived for two weeks, until we found permanent accommodation.

In the beginning all went well. As soon as I had permission to work, I started to work. My first job was cleaning. I was working all night from 11:00 p.m. until 7:30 a.m. cleaning a school. By 4:00 a.m., my feet would be swollen and I almost could not take a single step. I worked on this job for over a year. After being so tired from not sleeping, I quit and looked for another job, a day job. I found a very good one in a boutique. I liked it very much because I love sewing, particularly making wedding dresses. I worked at the boutique for almost two years. I had a problem there, though, because the owner also drank, which was terrible because I drank with her several times. She also spent more money than she made and gradually went bankrupt. She owed money to many people and could not pay her employees. Finally, everything was taken away from her, she went out of business and closed the shop. Once again I had to look for work. I was lucky and found something quickly — a job in a factory sewing working clothes. My task was to make 150 of these items per day. After three months, if one was unable to complete the daily task, one was fired. They called it "piece work." Eventually, my quota increased and I had to sew up to 180 pieces of working clothes per day, and no more than that. I started at 7:00 a.m. and by 3:00 p.m. I would be dead because I had to work non-stop to come up with the amount they demanded. Nevertheless, I worked in that factory for over two years. But, as you know, my health was breaking down and I had to quit.

During my first year in Canada, I wasn't drinking as much. Almost nobody knew about it, I controlled myself very well. And then one day, the telephone rang and it was a cousin calling from Nicaragua with bad news. One of my sons, the youngest one, had killed himself. This was a terrible shock to me. All I could think of at that moment was that day four years ago when I left Nicaragua, leaving him behind with tears in his eyes. He was fourteen years old then. He took his life at eighteen years old. I could not go to see him, not even for his funeral, because I did not have my papers and could not leave Canada. How I suffered, and still suffer. I felt responsible for his death. I began to drink again more frequently, because I thought that it was a way to forget. But it is not true; my remorse and my pain are still alive within me. Even less than a year after my son's death, I received more bad news — my oldest son had also died, in an ambush, and his body could not be recovered because he died in Honduras. My remorse became even greater, because I understood that due to my alcoholism I had not known how to be a good mother.

I know that my daughter has suffered very much. I had many problems with her — on one occasion I even told her to get out of the house because she threw away a bottle and that made me furious. When I was sober again, I would ask her to forgive me. Since she was so nice and good, she always forgave me. She is now at university and her dream is to become an excellent lawyer — she wants to study international law. I always advise her not to stop until she achieves what she wants, because the only thing that matters in this life is learning, and those who do not know anything have no other choice than being a beast of burden for those who do know.

I have survived my sickness. Sure, I also had problems with my jobs, because many times I missed work and I always told them a lie to justify my absence. Many times I said that my mother had died, which was a lie, since my mother died over twenty years ago. She was never aware of my alcoholism and it is better this way because she would have suffered a lot; the worst part of this sickness is that one brings pain to their loved ones. Thank God the problem with alcoholism has been disappearing little by little, but, it is very hard. Only someone who has this problem or sickness knows that one suffers, but it is something that cannot be helped. An alcoholic says, "I am not going to drink," and before she is aware of it, the same thing happens again. Worst of all, an alcoholic continues drinking until the body can no longer endure it. But afterwards comes the depression and the guilt for what she has done and then she swears over and over never to drink again. But what is inside the blood is stronger and she can only be cured with the help of God and through personal will power. I ask myself whether many others have found a cure on their own, with only God's help, because I could not do it. And now this is my goal, to cure myself and to help others who are afflicted.

Today, I am working in a home for people with mental and physical disabilities. I am happy to be able to help them, even a little, because at that place there are also people who have my problem. I have gone for over five years without drinking a single drop of alcohol and I feel happy. When I remember all the mistakes that I made in the past, I feel bad, but what can I do? I cannot erase the past. Now I try to move forward and to make up for all the damage that I have done, both to my health and to the people I love. Because, even if you may find it hard to believe, I do feel guilty for what happened to my sons. I think that if I had not had this illness, maybe things would have been different and perhaps my sons would have lived. For an alcoholic the urge to drink is stronger than anything. And that is why I rely upon my faith in God, because I do not want to destroy my daughter's life, as I destroyed the life of my other children.

My daughter tells me, "You see, Mom, how different everything is when you're well. I am happy and I can concentrate on my studies, but when you're sick, I cannot concentrate, I can only think about your problem and how long it is going to last." I have promised her for the last time that, for as long as I live, I will make her happy and I will never drink again. Somehow, I will compensate for what she has suffered because, despite my drinking episodes, she has always looked after me and helped me and understood me. Another person in her place would have left and would not have put up with me for as long as she has done. But she goes on loving me and even more now that I am "almost cured." I do not say "cured" because that is something that an alcoholic can never be. This sickness is deceiving and when you least expect it, you fall back into it again.

I think that I have taken a big step forward and hope that my story will be useful to those who are still drinking, so that they might think about it. This sickness makes a person sink deeper and deeper every day, until you finally fall into an abyss from which it is almost impossible to climb out. Luckily, I knew when to stop, before touching the bottom, because when you touch the bottom, it is too late to get up again. And this is the reason that when I am tempted to drink, I begin to remember the past and the bitter days I lived through and say, "NO, I do not want to go back to that again, it is enough, I must be strong." I have been keeping myself sober for five years. I hope to continue being strong until the end.

One more thing, people like me, who have this problem, need understanding and love, because sometimes the depression is so deep that alcoholics take their lives. Their families may despise them or throw them out into the street, without understanding that they are human beings with a terrible disease. And that is humanity's biggest mistake, because what alcoholics need is affection and understanding. If someone in trouble receives affection when needed, she might feel happy, and deep down inside might promise to make an effort to cure herself. But if someone is despised, or kicked out into the streets, it is worse because then, deep down inside she thinks, "Why should I stop drinking if nobody loves me, if nobody cares about me?" A person who suffers from this evil needs a lot of affection and understanding. My daughter always supported me; she never left me to cope on my own and that was the best medicine for me.

Here in Canada I have worked a lot. Sure, I have lost many of my jobs because of my illness and that is why I am now making an effort to get over it. Now I want to succeed in my work. I have my own business designing custom-made clothes for women and doing alterations. I would also like my daughter to succeed. I would like to support her as she has supported me. I also want to help those who are suffering from the depression and the remorse of alcoholism. I often wonder whether my life would have been different if I had never suffered from this evil. Nevertheless, here in Canada I have met people who have supported me and understood me and I am very happy now because I feel that I have been able to overcome this problem. When I see that my daughter is happy and is studying very hard, I feel even more strength to move ahead and, perhaps, one day, bring my other sons to Canada. Then I would be complete, here, in this country which has given me warmth, affection and understanding. I remember the day I stepped onto this glorious land, when I felt like one of those little bunnies, all scared because I could not understand a word of English and everything was so strange to me. But now, every-thing looks so familiar that even the snow seems beautiful to me and I think that I could never live away from this country, particularly because of my daughter. She is happy here at the university and she also feels as if she has lived here all her life.

Today I am working with people who are not well and I feel that I am doing something useful by helping them. Many of them are young and I think this illness might destroy their lives. Alcoholism not only destroys the people who suffer from it, it also destroys those around them. I hope that whoever reads this story and who might suffer from this illness can better understand its consequences, reflect a little and make an effort to abandon this terrible habit. I know that it is difficult, but not impossible if you have the will power. Nobody can cure you except yourself. And when that happens, you will feel liberated and happy to be useful again and not to be a parasite any longer. What I have told here is only a part of my life, but I hope that it proves to be useful, so that you may think that there is nothing more wonderful in life than having a family and good health.

Translated from the Spanish by Marcela Leighton Krautter.

Looking for What?

TRACY FRANKLIN

I start my day
asking for guidance
knowledge, willingness

I go through my day
forgetting what I
yearned for
making mistakes, questioning
analyzing

I end my day
apologizing
again asking for
the things of the morn
crying sometimes

Praying
I have another
chance
tomorrow

Being a Single Mom

ALEXANDRA

Ring! Ring! Ring! The alarm rings and it's 6:15. Luckily, I set my alarm for twenty minutes earlier than I need to get up. This allows me to hit the snooze button two or three times. I jump, or rather crawl, out of bed, turn on the kettle for my morning coffee and drag myself to the bathroom for a quick shower. I drink my coffee while dressing, fixing my face and hair, while my son still sleeps. I fix my lunch, get my school bag ready and put my shoes on. The next step is to awaken my four-year-old son, Dylan. I have to do it three to four times as he turns over, covers his face with the blankets and mutters and complains, "Go away, I'm tired." Eventually Dylan awakens, goes to the washroom, brushes his teeth and hair and dresses himself (no buttons, for they hurt when he's hugged). At 7:30 a.m., we walk or run to Dylan's daycare, about five minutes from our apartment. Dylan eats his breakfast at daycare and spends most of his day there. It's in a grade school, so he'll probably go there until Grade Eight. I drop him off and literally run to catch the 7:45 bus outside the school.

During the days, Monday to Friday, I attend college where I am enrolled in a two-year Early Childhood Education Program. I spend my day either in school or in placements. I plan to do my third year at university and receive my degree in ECE. When the school day's finished, I catch two buses, walk to Dylan's school and pick him up. Depending on my schedule this could be anywhere between 2:00 p.m. and 6:00 p.m. The evening consists of cleaning up the apartment, making dinner and doing the dishes, spending time with Dylan. Every other night he has a bath. He gets his pyjamas on and is in bed reading with lights on at 8:30 p.m. I turn the lights off, we say our prayers and Dylan listens to lullabies. He is asleep by 9:00 or 9:30. Of course when we add extra activities, our schedule changes. On Saturdays I work five to eight hours and Dylan is watched by his grandma and grandpa. On Sunday mornings we attend the 9:30 worship service and the 11:00 church service, and Bible study on Sunday nights. Sunday is a day of naps, church and laundry at Grandma's. One night a month we do our grocery shopping.

Dylan is about a year behind in his speech and has been assigned to the local hospital for speech therapy. We are lucky to be in the program for the waiting list is one year. A team from Dylan's daycare and our families work together to help Dylan overcome his problem. Dylan has come a long way and all agree that he is very willing to learn.

When I was a child I lived in a dysfunctional home. Of course I didn't realize this until I was older and had to work through many problems. Over the last four years I have had to review my life and give forgiveness for the wrong that has been done to me, as well as ask forgiveness for my part in the problems or situations I have caused.

I was raised in a traditional home where the father was the head of the household. He worked, he provided for the family, he disciplined the family, he made all the decisions. My mother was obedient, quiet and submissive. She backed my father in all areas, whether she agreed or not. My father was raised in a bad home — his mother died at his birth and his father was an alcoholic. My father was very authoritarian. He worked hard and was often helping others in the community rather than helping us at home. When I was five, my mother suspected him of having an affair, but he chose to stay with us. For the next five years, he went to college and graduated with honours as an ambulance attendant. The house was still ruled and controlled by him. My mother started her own daycare to pay the school bills and other costs for a home and family. We children were expected to remain quiet to allow my father to study. When I was ten years old, my father left us — four days after my parents' seventeenth anniversary. He moved in with his future second wife, where he has stayed till this day. We kids made regular weekend visits and for a time I was allowed to phone my father collect at anytime. This soon changed.

Life changed for me after my father left. I never understood how, since I was never close to him. We were so much alike in our temperaments and moods that we did not get along at all. When he moved out I lost all forms of discipline and rules in my life. My mother and older sister had their own troubles adjusting to the separation and divorce. Eventually, in Grade Nine, I moved in with my father, my stepmother and my one-year-old half brother. I moved because my mother and sister had trouble dealing with my temperament and moods; I blamed them for everything. Due to my anger, I had no friends, no family (or so I felt) and very bad grades. While I lived with Dad, I fell into a "bad crowd." I was accused of drinking, having premarital sex and taking drugs. These accusations were wrong. The situation at my father's grew worse each day. We were learning that we too had problems. My father and stepmother never got along on the best of days. We attended family counselling at Children's Aid and at a hospital clinic. My father and stepmother were convinced that I was trying to split them up as well as hurt my half brother. They believed I was unstable and depressed. This was true to some extent. I felt unwanted, undesirable and unlovable. One day we found out that we were moving to a new house. To give you a good idea of the family dynamics, neither my father nor I knew we were moving until we saw the For Sale sign on the lawn. We didn't see the new house until we moved in.

In Grade Ten I started going to a new school and made a new bunch of friends. Tension at home grew worse by the day. My father continued to be very authoritarian. My curfew was moved up. I wasn't allowed in my room except to sleep. No television for more than one hour. Home became very rule-bound. Then abuse crawled into the situation and my attitude changed. I began to run away. I always came back. During my stepmother's second pregnancy, I ran away again and this time I was not welcomed back. We agreed I would live in a women's shelter until I could move into a girls' group home. I lived in the group home one month. My emotional state was terrible, I was depressed, suicidal, rejected and alone. I had been punished and disciplined for so long for things I was suspected of that I no longer cared. I took part in everything I was accused of doing — drugs, sex and alcohol. After being kicked out of school and the group home I moved into a one-bedroom apartment with two friends.

The next month or two were a blur. I was into everything from drugs to prostitution. I was out on the streets and vulnerable. I was an emotional wreck. I attempted suicide more times than I can or care to remember. I was raped once and beat up a few times. That summer, my mom allowed me to move home. By this time I wasn't speaking to my stepmother or my father or his two sons. My mother had remarried as well. I stayed at home for a few months and then moved to an apartment in a friend's home. I dropped out of school once again and "fell in love." In November I moved in with my boyfriend, who wanted only one thing. At this point I was so low, so depressed, so suicidal and rejected that I felt I had no one. I thought a child would answer all my problems. So I planned to get pregnant. In December I found out that I was four to six weeks pregnant. My boyfriend was not happy. In April we broke up and I moved back home. In May he lost his job and his apartment, and his family offered to pay his way back to the Maritimes; he left.

During my pregnancy I gained fifty pounds, and on August 21, 1991, I gave birth to a healthy nine-pound five-ounce baby boy. I lived at home for the next three years, finishing high school with honours and attending the first year of Child and Youth at college. In October of Dylan's third year I moved out to a two-bedroom and had a full-time job at a program called LINC, which teaches English to newcomers to Canada. I worked in the child minding section and enjoyed it very much. My supervisor and I learned that in order for LINC to have a daycare we would need a qualified ECE worker. She suggested I go back to college part-time, so I agreed. Unfortunately, when I started college in the fall, my school hours did not match my hours for work. I had to leave my job, and I left on good terms. I have been enjoying the program at college immensely. Due to cutbacks in the social services, though, I needed to have a part-time job. Fortunately my social assistance now covers my rent and phone bill, insurance and cable. My part-time job allows for all grocery bills and extras. I save my GST refunds, baby bonus and income tax for "rainy days" or for clothing that Dylan or I may need.

When I planned to get pregnant, I knew what I was getting into. I knew it would mean being accountable and responsible in all ways — physically, emotionally, spiritually, financially — for twenty-two years. I'm not surprised at anything now; my wish has come true and I wouldn't trade Dylan for anything. I love him very much and I only want the best for him. My one regret is that my son will never have his biological father. He will have financial struggles and he may always have his doubts about who his father is.

I believe if it was not for the stability that Dylan has brought to my life I would not be here right now. I have learned throughout the last four years that a planned child or pregnancy will not give me happiness. A child should not be expected to provide the happiness or stability to a parent, this is what the child deserves to receive from the parent. I'm glad that I have my son, but being a single young mom is not a choice or a decision that I would make again. I look forward to the day when I am stable in all ways, happy and married and planning for more children with my husband.

My Healing Journey

MARGARET THOMAS

I've always wanted to tell my story. I've had this desire to talk or write about my history because I've learned so much on my healing journey.

I was the seventh child out of ten. My parents separated when I was five years old. I grew up on a Native reserve with inadequate food and clothing and went to school on the reserve up to Grade Eight. I had to go off the reserve for high school, which was a shock and a big adjustment. But in my own mind I always knew there would be hurdles to overcome in order to survive. I didn't want my children to grow up knowing the hardships I experienced. And I understand the values of my mom and how she raised us. I give a lot of credit to my mom because she went through hard times in order to keep us together. She strongly and repeatedly told us, "Never depend on any man to take care of you. Make sure you can take care of yourself."

By the time I was in my teens I already had it planned out. I knew I was going to complete high school. I knew I was going to college. And I did. And I also knew I was going to live common-law before I decided to marry. I had it set in my own mind that I was going to have children in my late twenties, which I did.

I had very rigid, very controlled goals that I wanted to accomplish, and I guess in many ways my partner had to fit into my goals and everything had to be done my way. I had to have so much control over my life because I didn't have control over it as a child.

I met and lived common-law with my partner when I was twenty years old. During this time, I went to college and received my certificate in the Child and Youth Worker Program. I then started working full-time with children in a treatment centre in Toronto. I worked so hard that I burnt myself out emotionally and physically, so I took time off to recover. Three months later, I started working in a group home for adolescent girls in Hamilton. I had to work because I didn't want to be financially dependent on anyone. When I established my independence, I married my partner. I was twenty-five years old.

Yet, after reaching all my goals, I was still unhappy inside. I always felt there was this great big hole inside of me. I asked my family doctor for a referral to a counsellor when I was twenty-six years old. I was pregnant with my first child. I wanted to know how to control my anger so that I wouldn't become an abusive parent. This was when I met Dr. Loys Ligate. During my pregnancy, I attended weekly therapy sessions to learn anger management. After I gave birth to Ashley, I stopped going. I had my second child at thirty, and my third child at thirty-three.

In 1989, my partner and I bought a new home near my reserve. Another part of my long-term plan was to eventually work with my own people. I guess my main focus was to try and help other people through the system that was not there for me as a child. On the reserve, I started working with women who were victims of abuse. When I worked as a counsellor, I heard many unique stories. One of the reasons that I went into therapy was that I knew that I had to have my own stuff worked out in order for me to help other women in the area of sexual abuse. I could work with women around family violence issues, but, when it came to sexual abuse, I had to resolve my own issues.

Another thing that triggered me into recognizing that I hadn't dealt with my past was when I heard John Bradshaw speak about sexual abuse at a workshop. He is the author of several books, including *Healing the Shame that Binds You.* I went to his workshop as part of my professional training. Up until that point I thought I was fine, there was nothing wrong with me. I remember walking out of the workshop and going outside. A therapist, I didn't get her name, followed me to make sure I was okay. I told her a bit about my memories of childhood sexual abuse. I always had the memories, but I had pushed them down inside. It was obvious that it was time to go back to therapy.

I confided in my co-worker, Gina, who supported my plan to go into therapy. I told her that I would only need three to four months and then I would be done. Today, Gina and I laugh about my unrealistic goal because she knew it would be longer. Gina has always been there for me, listening, caring and accepting me unconditionally. She has a big warm heart and for the first time, I have a very special friend.

So I called up Loys and I met with her in Toronto. I was back in therapy once a week at age thirty-four. When I started back, I said to her, "You know you're going to be my surrogate mother, because even though I have a mother, I don't have the emotional part — the nurturing, the affection, the caring." My mother does what she can, in her own little ways, but it's not direct. Every time I saw Loys she would give me a hug at the end of our meeting. I would never say, "No, I don't want a hug,"

I would just let her do it and I would numb out. I didn't feel anything. It was a long time before I told her that. So she asked me if it was best to stop the hugs and I said no. I said, "Eventually I am going to feel something, but right now I don't feel anything." So it took a really long time I think to get through it all, to start to feel deep emotion and to feel pain. By re-living everything, I had to go back through the pain. I had to go back and look at all those issues — the pain, the hurt, the anger, the resentment and betrayal. The lack of protection.

At the beginning, I had talked about way back when I was really young, when things started for me — when I was five years old, the very first time I was raped. The sexual abuse continued from the time I was five to when I was seventeen years old. There never seemed to be a time period when I wasn't being sexually violated or molested by a male. It seemed to be the normal thing that happened, whether it was abuse by a trusted male or by neighbours or incest with cousins. No one told us it was wrong. If the trusted adults were having pleasure from me as a child, why would it be any different to have incest with cousins? It was the only pleasant physical affection that I had been exposed to in childhood. So you can imagine what it was like to find out that was taboo.

And so, when I was seventeen and sexually assaulted, I never told anybody what happened to me, because I didn't think anyone would believe me. A famous family had come into town and a bunch of us went to see them perform. Afterwards, there was a dance where I felt set up. The brother of the famous person had set it up so it looked like I was going along with him on the dance floor as he started kissing me. I mean, because I had been victimized for so many years with the sexual abuse, I had no boundaries, I didn't know that I could say no. He asked me to go on their tour bus. He showed me inside the bus; I felt he had manipulated a naive seventeen-year-old into performing sex on him, which I considered to be another rape. That was the last time anyone has ever done anything to me as far as sexual assault. I don't know how or why, it just didn't happen after that.

For me there was a lot of denial. The memories were there, I knew what had happened to me, but I didn't have the emotional part of it. So I could tell Loys about the incidents without feeling anything. Or sometimes I would just sit there and cry. Sometimes I couldn't even talk about it, but the pain would be there. I did a lot of crying over the years. Today I look at it as a grief process. I had to re-live everything that happened to me as a child, to go through the memories again, to heal the scars. A lot of the time I felt like I was walking around with this big open wound, like an open sore and everybody could see it and everybody could recognize what was going on inside me — the loneliness, the emptiness.

Loys would say, "You know, Margaret, you need to start building something with your sister." I was lucky to have a sister who had not gone through the same things that I had been through. I chose her because we had protected each other during our childhood. She also had wisdom and a strong spiritual belief. She had the positive memories that I didn't have. I remember one day telling her that she had to be my positive memory bank. We grew up in a family where there was no affection, no verbal caring for one another. It's really hard for me to show any kind of feelings towards my family because I didn't grow up with it. It's something you just don't do.

It was so important to have her believe in me and to understand why I was different from her. She used to always question why I was so full of anger and why I was so mean. I always felt I was the "bad twin" and she was the "good twin." It wasn't easy to get her to listen to me or for me to share all my shameful secrets, but I did it because I was determined to have her understand me as a person and to gain her support throughout my healing process. My sister acknowledged and validated my pain when she gave me a card and a plaque with a poem on it that encouraged me to believe in our Creator, to believe he is there when I need him the most to heal me through my pain and suffering.

I don't want to hurt my family in any way and I don't want to use names of my family members, but I think it's important to recognize my sister, Reva, who painfully listened to me and has always been there when I needed her support.

During my time in therapy, I also went back to having eating problems, the way I did when I was growing up. Sometimes I would go for a long time without eating. Sometimes I would do the purging. And I think it was because I was beginning to feel, to learn how to feel inside. Because the feelings and the pain were so intense, the only thing I had control over was what went in my mouth and what came out. I felt like I was losing control in that sense. It took me back to when I was thirteen years old — I have pictures of me then, and I was really skinny. I had diarrhea for years. Everyday, I remember I'd have to get up early just to go to the bathroom and wait until my stomach settled and hope that I made the bus on time.

When I was back in therapy, the same thing started to happen again. Every time I'd drive to see Loys in Toronto, I'd have severe stomach cramps and pains, and by the time I got there, I had to run to the bathroom. This went on for a long time, maybe two years, every Friday morning. I ended up in the hospital for five days. They told me I had a bowel obstruction. Then more tests were done and they found out it wasn't a bowel obstruction but irritable bowel syndrome, which is caused by stress. The specialist asked me about my past and my history. I told him I was a victim of sexual abuse and I think to a great extent, it was the same problem I had as a teenager — that's why I was so skinny. My body was physically reacting to the painful memories that I was bringing out in therapy.

After I recovered and left the hospital, I continued struggling through my weekly therapy sessions. I developed more effective ways to take care of my body. I decided to join a gym to maintain better control of my weight, because I wasn't happy with my body. When I first started, I went seven days a week, which became my next compulsive act. I felt so out of control trying to learn the aerobic and step-class moves. Plus, there were mirrors from one end of the room to the other. I'd do my thing in the back of the class because I felt like a fool out of control, and I didn't want to see my body or my image in the mirrors. The sexual abuse left me feeling self-conscious and ashamed of my body. In my mind, I wanted to look good, but I had never worked at any physical exercise.

The mirrors became therapeutic as I started to look at my body form. My reflection helped me to accept my body image, and the more I worked out, the better I looked in the mirror. Then I started weight lifting, which improved all the "loose ends." After a year, the gym's owner asked me to pose for her advertisement in the local newspaper, and I felt honoured. Physical conditioning improves my self-esteem and it also works off stress and builds up my energy. I'm not so compulsive anymore, but I go on a regular basis because I like feeling physically fit.

After I work out, I can think more clearly emotionally so that I can better understand why I had to go through what I did. There has to be a reason, just as there has to be a reason for the everyday conflicts or encounters. I have the choice either to learn something from conflict or to hold onto the resentment and anger. It's difficult sometimes and my old coping mechanisms want to come back, but with me I guess my choice is not to do that anymore. Not to fall back into my eating disorders. Emotionally, I can cope much more effectively on a daily basis. Once you find that balance between the emotional, physical, spiritual and mental, it is so much easier to cope with everyday challenges. I feel a lot more inner peace.

Spiritually, I always had my own beliefs, but I think I suppressed my spirituality along with my other experiences. As a child, my mother always made sure that we went to our Longhouse ceremonies on a regular basis. I learned about the religious ceremonies from watching; however, I never fully understood the meaning of the ceremonies because I never learned the Native language. My mother understood three different Native languages. She had been conditioned through her experience in the residential schools that it wasn't okay to speak her language. Throughout my childhood experiences, I learned to believe in a higher power, our Creator. But when I was old enough I decided that I didn't want to go to the Longhouse anymore and that nobody could make me go. So I pushed that aside; I didn't believe in anything.

I think what really helped me spiritually was my grandmother's death. I was about thirty-six years old when she died. She was always around when I was growing up and I have a lot of feelings for her. She wasn't the affectionate, caring, typical grandmother type. She was very much like my mother. They showed that they cared about you in their own little ways, but they never told you physically or verbally that they cared about you. My grandmother had been pretty healthy but then she had a stroke. She decided it was time for her to go to the Creator.

She wanted to spend her time with her family at home and not in a hospital. She was at my aunt's home. She couldn't eat because of the stroke. She didn't want to eat. But she made it to her birthday and we had a party. That was the last time I can remember my grandmother sitting up and being alert as she watched everyone and her favourite soap opera. After that she was in bed most of the time. During that time I had to learn to accept that my grandmother was going to die, that it was her choice. She lived a full life. And it was her choice to go to the Creator.

Spiritually, I felt my grandmother's inner strength to make that decision. It's part of the whole life cycle — you're born, you come into this world and you have a whole life to live, and at some point in time you go to the Creator. My grandmother made the choice when she was ready to go. That was hard. I think for the first time, out of all the deaths in my family, I really felt the hurt and the pain of someone dying. And watching her, actually watching her. I was there when she died. I saw her spirit come out of her body when she took her last breath; I felt that the spirit was coming out and that my grandmother was finally on her journey to our Creator.

Going through that with my grandmother really helped me take a good look at life. I guess spiritually I knew that I had to believe in my own religious beliefs, in what I was raised with in the Longhouse in order to cope with life and work through grief. I don't know if I'm going to be here today or tomorrow. I don't know if my kids or my partner or my family are going to be with me for the next thirty years. Life is so precious that you can't take it for granted. I can't change what I've been through, I can only heal the scars and work through them. And there has to be a reason I was put through what I was put through. For me the answer is that I have the strength to survive.

I had the courage to go back into therapy and re-live all that, to understand, to learn, so that I could help other women — by being there for them, by listening, by understanding and by not being judgemental.

The turmoils that occur in my life today can be just as painful and difficult to experience; however, I have learned new ways to cope: by using self-care techniques and by turning to my friends who are very supportive. Friends who have been through what I've gone through can relate the most to my pain, since they too have experienced the same feelings.

Mentally, I still have Loys. She's there whenever I need her. If things build up, I know that I can go and get the support I need from her. She has been a very good surrogate mother. She has really nurtured me for about eight years. She has really cared about the things that I've had to deal with. Often, I wanted to shove her away and tell her not to care about me. But no matter what I did and no matter what I said to her she never pushed me away. She kept on. She stayed there for me and helped me through all those difficult issues. And she's still there; I know she'll always be there, if I need to see her. I'm sure it hasn't been easy for her. I don't think I'd want to be my therapist!

Today, I'm in a supervisory position. I don't do one-to-one counselling with women. I do staff supervision and administration. It's important to me to empower the staff, for us to feel that we have to work as a team. I may be a supervisor but that doesn't make me any better or any different than anybody else. I believe that there has to be equality, no matter what position you hold. We need to earn respect, we need to show respect, we need to be honest, we need to be up front with others. If we don't have a healthy team, then we're not going to help the people who come in for support. A healthy team is really important working in this kind of field, when we hear about sexual abuse and mental abuse and see the bruises. It's really tough. When we work with someone for a couple of years and then go to see them in the hospital, black and blue, that's really tough. There is a place and time when we need to be there for that woman, but we also need to take time to deal with our own feelings. So, I encourage all the women who work here to have a support system, whether it's a friend or a therapist, it's important that they have somebody to talk to about their feelings.

You hear a lot about men who abuse. Being a survivor of abuse, I believe I have resolved a lot of my feelings towards the "perpetrators." For me, it's important that we try to help the men as well, because if we don't help the men in our community then we're not going to stop the violence against women. These men who are abusing others have been abused themselves. Nobody was there for them when they were children. As an adult you have a choice whether to continue that behaviour or stop that behaviour, but how can they stop it without someone to help them? That's the other important part — to help families work through these issues, to keep families together if possible. I think in our Native community you can trace the violence back to the abuse of the residential schools; abuse has become a multi-generational cycle. Somebody once asked me how Native people used to deal with sexual abuse. I said, "Well, we never had sexual abuse in our culture. It can be traced back to residential schools."

The other significant point is that I don't ever want any of my own children to be sexually abused. I have tried to teach my kids about their own bodies. I taught them the body parts, especially my daughter, who is the oldest. I've spent time telling her about my childhood and how she can protect herself.

My daughter triggered feelings in me when she was five, six and seven. That's around the time I went back to therapy. I would get her ready for a bath and I would think as I looked at her, how could anybody do these things to a small child? I just couldn't imagine it, so I told her that no one had the right to touch her.

When my son was five years old, he started acting out sexually. At first we thought it was normal child exploration, but then it became more severe. There were several incidences that indicated he knew more about adult sex than any five-year-old should know about. His sexual acting out got to the point where I knew something was wrong. Following another serious incident that occurred in our home, I was so shocked and scared that I couldn't think clearly, and all my triggers from childhood came back. I called Loys for support and we agreed she would call the Children's Aid Society. The CAS interviewed my son, but they were not able to get anywhere. Again, he continued the sexual acting out; after each incident I would ask him to tell me where he learned this behaviour, but he would never tell. Six months later, I called the CAS because my son said he was ready to talk to the worker again.

I had always thought that if anybody ever abused my child, I'd want to kill them. But when it actually happened, I didn't feel that way. I didn't want to kill the man who did this to my child. I was in shock when the CAS worker reported that my son said it was the baby sitter's husband. The CAS and the police interviewed the man and when they called me back, they said he was genuine in his response. They felt that he was telling the truth when he said he did not abuse my son. I said, "Yeah, he's an adult. He can tell you what he needs to tell you and he can show you what he needs to show you to prove that he's genuine. I have a five-year-old boy who doesn't know how and cannot show it." They were accepting the adult's word against my five-year-old son's because he couldn't remember times and places. And his story was inconsistent. So they decided that my son didn't have a legitimate story. They believed the allegations were false, but in my heart I knew children at that age don't lie. I was five when I was raped.

What was important was to try to help my child through the therapy process to heal his scars. There was no point in being revengeful because it was a waste of energy. There was nothing I could do about the man. I could not change the fact that my son was sexually abused. If I gave into my old anger and hatred, I would be back to the physical and medical problems. Why worry about things that I had absolutely no control over? In the past several years, my son has shown positive signs of healing, and we have developed a very special emotional connection in many ways.

I've spent so many years being so negative, having gone through so much trauma, having to re-live all the pain, having lived so many years with so much anger, resentment and hatred. When you work through all that and when you let that kind of stuff go, it's such a big relief. Maybe I can live the next thirty years of my life without having to have that anger all the time. And that big empty hole that I talked about, I feel like it has finally been filled. Nobody could fill it for me — I had to do it myself. I had to fill that hole. I had to start caring about myself. I had to learn to accept me as I am. With everything that I've been through, even with my son, I have learned to let go of things that are beyond my control.

When I go to bed at night, I think about my day, I think about the good things that have happened. And if something negative has happened, a conflict or whatever, I try to figure out what is it that I want to gain from it, what my role is, what is or isn't my responsibility. I try to keep my boundaries clear.

The only time I am not very positive is when I have premenstrual syndrome (PMS). My kids are funny. I'll say to one of them, "Your mom has PMS," and he'll go running down the hallway yelling, "Mommy has PMS, stay out of her way!" So I do have my bad days once a month. Oh, god, they are awful. But when I have a headache and a sore back, if I feel bloated and miserable and ready to tear off someone's face, I know I have to try and control my behaviour. I warn the kids that I'm not in a very good mood. And they're really good. They know they cannot push it with me.

I live a busy lifestyle, always on the run. My day starts at 6:30 a.m. I have to get ready, then get my boys and my daughter out of bed. Deal with their moods in the morning. By 8:30 a.m. everyone is usually where they are supposed to be, at school and at work. It's like switching modes: you're a parent for two hours and when you walk into work, all of a sudden you're not a parent any longer. Your thinking is geared differently for seven and a half hours, sometimes longer. I enjoy what I do, it's always different. It's a challenge. The women and men who work together take their time to laugh and joke, which is therapeutic. Whenever anyone needs emotional support, there's always someone there. So it's really nice to go to work.

At the end of the day, my partner picks up our children and goes home to prepare dinner. I usually drive home, enjoying the peace and quiet between work and home. Spending time with my family is important. I want to know what has happened to them in their day and to make sure that they are okay. After dinner, I take time to myself by going to work out and to socialize with other women in the club. When I get home, it's bedtime routine. I try to be sleeping by 11:00 p.m.

I think it's important to have a partner who is going to give fifty percent of helping out with all the responsibilities. When both of us work full-time and with three children, it's not an easy life to do all the work alone. It's hard sometimes to keep the balance, but there will always be obstacles to overcome.

I would like to thank my friend, confidante and co-worker Gina, also my sister Reva for supporting and for encouraging me to write my story; my "surrogate mother," Dr. Loys Ligate, for all her unconditional giving and caring in teaching a terrified child to become a mature woman; my friend, Janice, for inspiring me in the physical workout and for hanging in there when things got tough. Thanks to Mary O'Connor for her gentleness and patience in listening to me tell my story. And last, but not least, thanks to my partner and my children for their support and unconditional love.

I would like to close with a special note to my mother: If you get to read my story one day, please know that if it weren't for you, I would never have had the opportunity to touch so many lives with my experiences. Thanks for giving birth to me and for keeping us together. No regrets.

A Child

TRACY FRANKLIN

There is anger
then she smiles
There is shame
then she holds out her hand to me

There is a huge loss of freedom
then I miss her
There is guilt
then she holds out her heart to me

There is frustration
then we share a special moment
There's so much love
then she holds out her whole life to me

She depends on me
loves me
frustrates and
angers me

I love her
need her
hold and take care of her
don't spend enough special time with her

Thank you, Lord, for the complexities of love and
all that it entails

Giving All That I Had to Give — And At What Cost?

MARIE SANSON

Let the beauty of what you love be what you do ...
— Sufi Poet, Rumi

In days gone by they would have called it a nervous breakdown and I would have been hospitalized for a time. Today, they call it being overcome by depression, with need for treatment of both depression and stress. No period of hospitalization is necessary — the wonderful drugs of the 1990s mask the symptoms and allow one to function.

My reality took place one summer day — and I didn't care what they called it. For me it was darkness, it was frightening, and I never thought I would find my way back to my life, to the world. It didn't happen instantly. It could have been an experience that was in the making all of my life, it could have resulted from my long history of work, or it could have been caused by the events that immediately preceded it. I suspect that it was all of these.

I do know that it was the dark night of my soul, that it was debilitating and that I never wish to have the experience again: the tears that wouldn't stop, the sensation for days and nights of dark clouds and then dark waves, which I fought and fought until I was too tired to fight any longer, finally succumbing to the dark waves that took me into a black hole. When I reached that place, I believed I would never again return to my life. The experience lasted for three days. I was home alone.

In some ways I can never return to my life as I knew it. Only those who have been there will understand what I mean. Those who are on the brink of going there will know enough to fear the journey, although they are probably not likely to be able to prevent it, any more than I was.

It is right to be afraid, because it is surely the worst and loneliest journey that one can take, next to death. There is no guarantee that the light will come again or that one can rely on one's strength to get through it all. Fortunately, I did find my way to the light and out of the dark.

My journey out was helped by the incessant ringing of the phone, by a dear friend miles away, who somehow knew that he was needed. So I grasped the edge of light that I found in that black hole of darkness, I answered the phone, and I began to understand that I was very ill. I had reached my physical, mental, emotional and spiritual limits. I was very human and vulnerable indeed.

I began the difficult process of recovery with assistance from friends and from God. I benefited from the help of a therapist, a doctor and medication. When the journey towards health felt too painful to bear, when I found myself unable to pray, one or several friends would reach out to me and support me, and I could steady myself again. I now know how to receive support. I know my limitations, I know I am not less strong because I am weak. I also know that I am a woman with much to give, and that it is okay that I cannot operate as a man in a man's world. Nor do I want to.

When I graduated from university, my first job introduced me to some of the harder realities of the world — violence, crime, premeditated evil, abuse — and to women who were afraid. I encountered many women whose identity as the spouse of someone in the criminal system was supremely important to them. It gave them status in their world. Some women were married to men who were "in" for life and lived in fear of them, even though the men were behind bars. Part of my job was to take these women to the penitentiaries to visit their husbands.

I worked with these women and I was greatly changed by them; I was greatly changed by the exposure to their stories and lives, stretching the boundaries of my own experience. Work wasn't just about work — it was also about radical personal change that would help me work more effectively. Passion and compassion arose in me.

I worked with their children. Some of the children lived with the same terror as their mothers, others had witnessed violence and abuse, and some had suffered abuse directly. My passion and compassion were combined with disbelief.

I had no preparation for what I saw and experienced and now worked with. University hadn't covered any of this. I operated from instinct and intellect. I attempted to help people find solutions where there were none. I was young enough to believe that if I only worked hard enough, lives could be saved. And so the long hours of work that were so hard emotionally and mentally and physically began. In those days, work supervision was rare. Those of us who were committed did our best. Salaries were low for this kind of work — after all, we were expected to be dedicated.

In my next job, I worked with children. Again, low pay, no supervision, long hours, draining work. But now I was driven — I could not turn my back on the evil and injustice for a job that might have been easier. I had made a commitment to do whatever I could to make the lives of children better. I witnessed more than a human being ever should. I saw children with bruises and broken limbs, cigarette burns on their buttocks and feet, head injuries requiring surgery. I witnessed horrible family scenes — yelling, verbal abuse, physical abuse. I apprehended children and took them to "safety," often to foster homes that harmed the children even more. Sometimes the parents would seek help and attempt to be better parents. Sometimes the parents were happy that their child was being apprehended — they didn't want the child. That was worse.

Over a ten-year period, I took hundreds of children into protection. I worked with the children, worked with the families, returned many to their homes and saw some of the children through adoption. I was verbally abused, physically threatened. I had guns pointed at me. I cried for the children, I cried for the families, and I cried for myself. Nothing could prepare me for what I saw and experienced. I know that some of the children lived to become adults because of my work. I also know their scars wouldn't go away. I know that in many, many heartbreaking situations there was little I could legally do. I supported, I counselled, I kept a vigilant eye, and something inside of me was deeply harmed at my helplessness in the face of so much abuse.

It would have been better if I had become hard and cynical — it wouldn't have hurt so very, very much. But it changed me radically, yet again. My compassion for the children and for some of their mothers grew. My passion to find a way to change society also grew. I needed to do something about my overwhelming sense of helplessness in view of all that I had seen.

Looking back, I know I no longer had a balanced perspective about life — I was exposed to the worst of what humanity could do to one another. I was aware of abuse or the signs of it wherever I went — the mall, the beach, the park. This awareness and deep caring about humanity was new for me. I had never before felt these feelings so deeply, and I had never before been so committed to working so hard.

During this time, I tried hard to keep a balance between my work and the rest of my life. My husband and I lived in the country. I insisted on being in nature as much as possible, I craved its healing. I spent a lot of time working in the garden, inhaling life from the plants, the sunshine, the rain, the soil. My husband resented the time and energy I put into my work. We had many fights that began with him asking why I couldn't or wouldn't just see it as a job. He said I was being exploited: I should be putting in my eight-hour days and spending the rest of the time at home. I couldn't see it that way. There was so much to be done. I was torn between the demands of my two worlds. My husband got angry when I brought my work concerns home. He began to dictate solutions to me without listening to me. I really just needed to talk. But that only made things worse so I tried to keep my struggles to myself. I listened to him go on by the hour about his work. Today, I don't know why I put up with this lack of mutuality. I suppose it was because that's how I saw a wife's role.

My mother also didn't want to hear about my work with "those welfare bums." She told me that I would ruin my marriage by putting so much of myself into my work. She said I had been encouraged to go to university not so that I could work, but so that I could find the "right husband." She had never imagined that I would choose a career. Her expectations for me were that I would be a good housewife.

I have several children. I love being a mother and enjoy immensely my relationship with them. I don't want to minimize how they sapped my strength — having them, nursing them, caring for them. To say nothing of the never-ending pile of laundry, the countless meals and the chauffeuring. They are, though, how I managed to keep my sanity. I cherish them and I know I am cherished by them. They remind me of the beautiful side of humanity.

We had bought a small house and built a huge house around it ourselves. Work at work and work at home. Against this backdrop I cooked, cleaned, did laundry, made jams and relishes and pickles, froze fruits and vegetables from the garden. During the years that building took us, I also did the lawn mowing and any other outside work that didn't take absolute brute strength. The day before one of my children was born, I remember pushing the gas mower for the five hours it took me to do two acres. My mother was there insisting we rake the grass.

Both my husband and my mother told me I should stay home and take care of the house and the children; they had very clear ideas of how that should be done. I wanted to be a good mother and to take care of the house. I no longer cared about being a good wife and daughter, because I could never meet the expectations anyway. I was very angry. But the jobs at home got done and I did the childcare arrangements myself. I worked hard outside the home, but made sure that nothing at home suffered as a result.

When my children were still quite young, I took a management job in the inner-city and worked with the homeless, the marginalized, with children and families living in poverty. The workload was enormous and never-ending. The injustice of society that I was now intimate with drove me to fight hard against it. It took a lot of energy, but I realized that in my job it was possible for me to get people to work together to help make changes. The fullness of what I experienced in this work, what I saw, cannot be captured here. There was so much need and only so much we could really accomplish. Yet there were things we did manage to achieve. Through these small achievements, I believe I have made some major changes in our community and have offered leadership to make our community a better place for all of its citizens. I am in awe of the position of privilege I have been able to hold to do this work. When I look back on this time, I will always see my greatest achievement (other than having my children) as the day a political committee in our community agreed that there were homeless on the streets of our city who were not there by choice. This realization was a major breakthrough.

I worked in this position for many years, giving it all that I had. It was incredibly demanding of my time, yet I continued to take care of my children and my home. During that time, however, my relationship with my husband became worse. He had become completely hostile towards me and my work. Then he became hostile towards the children. I put up with his anger and rage as long as I could. But our home had become very unsafe. My husband blamed his right to his anger on me and my love of my work. Finally, I decided to leave him. The children and I moved to a home of our own. We needed a home that was safe. It was hard to leave the home I had helped build, my garden. And it wasn't any easier for the children. Now my husband and I are separated. There will be no reconciliation. I am still working out the results of the manifestation of his anger. But now the children and I are safe. It's hard to make it on one salary with no child support, but we'll do it.

My mother was against my leaving my husband. During the first few years of our separation, she would visit and give me a hard time about how I was raising my children. She took a strong stand against their behaviour. I suggested we talk about it. But she refused to. And one day she hit one of my children across the mouth for using poor manners at the table. She hasn't talked to any of us since then. She said that if I hadn't put my career before my children, that they would be better behaved. When she walked out like that, I felt anger at her for letting me down.

Despite what my mother says, I think the children have turned out beautifully. Their self-esteem is good, they understand that they have a right to be safe and to have their needs met and that they have a responsibility to each other and to me. I feel excited as I watch them head into their futures. And their manners will do. I am proud of my children and love them deeply and am thankful for every minute with them.

I have survived much, I have accomplished much, I have withstood much. But I write this story on the night before I tender my resignation at my workplace. What finally got me down was not the demands of my home life and family. It was not the demands of the work I do, although these demands have been great and many times I have been exhausted. It was not the challenge of coping with my mother and husband who fought me all the way. Although all of these did play a part. In the end, it was the harassment I endured at work that has brought me to my knees.

The harassment took place when I was in a position of authority. The man who harassed me was part of our management team and held a position of power over me. I felt helpless, and couldn't figure out where to turn. I put up with his behaviour for several months. That's when I collapsed and stopped going to work. At that point I was even incapable of caring for my children. Someone had to come and take care of them.

The blackness of the breakdown was beautiful oblivion for a while. Then I moved out of my despair and went back to work, and I raised the issue with my colleagues. The sexual harassment stopped, there was mediation (one session — he didn't have time to go again). A few months later, he met with me and told me that if I didn't write a letter of apology saying that there had been no harassment and that I only said it because of stress, that I would pay for it. Needless to say, I didn't write the letter. The harassment by this man resumed, and went on for several months. I couldn't carry on my job without encountering him. I have no idea why he targeted me. Did I stand in his way? Was it because I am a woman who was in a position of authority?

The stress has been terrible. I can't fight it anymore. I am tired. I can't put myself in the position of having another breakdown. I will resign and walk away. And then I'll sort out what I'm going to do with the rest of my life. I hope to find a job soon, though. I have children and myself to support. With the rest of my life I will be the gift that I am, live the truth that I am with compassion, loyalty, love, wisdom, passion and humour.

Untold Secrets

BERNADETTE ALPEN

Like the opening of the *Twilight Zone*, "somewhere in another dimension, another time," this is what happened to one family and how it was never the same again.

Somewhere in Canada, in the late 1970s, I chose "life." I kept the child I was carrying. A son was born. Alone, I embarked on a journey to continue my education in the childcare field. Through trial and error, I found capable people to nurture and care for my son while I learned about child development.

Working on homework papers and preparing for workshops after my son was in bed didn't leave much time for a social life outside college. Unexpectedly, an opportunity arose to enjoy an evening out with another college student. She was just getting to know a fellow and needed the moral support only a girlfriend can provide. I was invited along. I wasn't nursing any longer and my mom and dad could come to baby sit. After a few other evenings as a threesome, I was introduced to a friend from out of town and a friendship evolved between us. Soon he became my husband-to-be.

College was almost over and my son who had just entered a play-school program, was having difficulty adjusting. He wasn't getting along with the other kids. After six weeks and many conference calls and notes home, I turned to my doctor for advice. Because I was a single parent, parenting courses were suggested. When I attended my first session, my son was two and a half; I had at my disposal many professionals in the field. So I asked questions about family support, stress, growing-up time and, because of my interest in early childhood development, I knew that children needed consistency and routine. I wanted to know whether I could adapt my own routine to improve his behaviour. Children generally take time to adapt to new routines, like daycare, and to changes in family life. When my son started in the play-school program, I had just started a new relationship with my husband-to-be. My son had to share me with him and this must have been hard for him to take. Many suggestions were given to my questions and concerns. I tried many, kept what worked and disregarded the rest.

Sometime later I started working in a daycare and was able to take my son along — he was in a younger group setting. We often did not see each other during the day, so we shared our day on the way home. But soon behaviour problems arose at that centre, too! I enrolled him in another centre with the understanding that we were all going to work on his problem behaviours, specifically his social and verbal skills.

In between the everyday routine of working and being a single parent I was seeing my husband-to-be and we often went out with friends we had in common. My friend who introduced us always had nephews and nieces over to her house, so we gravitated there, too. Over time my husband-to-be and I shared concerns about my son's behaviour in a caring, loving way. My being a first-time parent and him an instant parent, we often talked long on the phone. After a time, we moved in together, and eventually we married.

We had good and bad days, like most parents, learning as we went along. I felt in a better position than my husband, since child development and behaviour was my "work." I had an edge on understanding the approaches to use with my son. The problem seemed behavioural more than psychological. At this time my son was nearly four and we needed to be around to supervise more than parents usually do with children this age. Sleeping was a problem, too; he didn't require much. Afternoon naps were out and this posed a problem at daycare. We took into consideration that our marriage would have required an adjustment for my son. Maybe this was contributing to his behaviour. By the time he was ready for Early Childhood Education registration, we figured that a teacher and a school would straighten him out — these would offer him a consistent environment and a routine.

Then Grade Two. I was lucky that the teacher he had took a special liking to him and gave him her full attention — something he had a hard time maintaining. She tried a variety of methods — rewards, discipline — all with our approval. Over that year, we also tried diet as a way of controlling his outbursts and hyperactivity. By now we had a new baby to consider as well, so my son's diet involved a budget adjustment to buy the dye-free, sugar-free and additive-free products. This helped somewhat. I also pursued a referral to a child psychologist, who told me the name for the disorder. My son had the popular one at the time: Attention Deficit Disorder (ADD). The disorder causes a defiance to authority, that is, the child shows no respect for other people's opinions or suggestions. Other symptoms include cruelty to animals, destruction of property, day dreaming, hyperactivity, inflexibility and manipulative behaviour. My pediatrician, who specialized with children with this disability, prescribed Ritalin, which had to be monitored. The medication helped my son be more attentive at school by slowing him down enough so he could learn. His social behaviour was ours to deal with.

There were books available on the subject and there were follow-up appointments to check the medication. By now we were parents of a six-year-old on Ritalin. The medication needed a few weeks to build up in his system. Over the next two years the improvement was minimal. We tried other medications, I even looked into a support group, as it seemed no one else in the school was having this problem but us. In spite of school confidentiality, I agreed that our name could be given out. But nothing came of it. I also attended many presentations given by speakers who were popular in the parenting field.

When my son was between Grades One and Three, our pediatrician sent us to a hospital's audiology department for an assessment. The audiologist diagnosed my son as having an auditory processing disability, which is also a symptom of ADD. I shared this information with the special education teacher at his school, so that she could guide and instruct his homeroom teacher. His Grade One teacher was eager to learn and work with my son and me. She could see the good in him and wanted to help. This was very reassuring at the time because up until then I had only been hearing negative comments about him. This set the wheels in motion for him to have a learning disability assessment by the school psychologist. I was put on the waiting list. When the time came, the psychologist made a home visit and the test went well. Recommendations were made for him to have an individual placement in the school system, which meant his work would be modified and monitored more closely. The assessment was also helpful because for the first time I learned that we were not alone with this problem.

During this time, I had taken a few daycare kids into my home to help my son by providing him with playmates and to earn extra money. I loved the independence of making my own money. I also made friends with the parents of the daycare children. Over the next few years, with new kids coming and going, I got to see different personalities and how a child's disposition makes a difference to learning. I enjoyed all my charges. I had a child with a speech delay, another with birth trauma and others with slight disabilities, so I was learning.

After our fourth child was born, our life grew more stressful. The behaviour of my oldest son needed more controlling from our end. He still had not learned to be reliable or as trustworthy as would have been expected of a boy his age. He was not invited to birthday parties and was aggressive at school. The school could only be so understanding. My husband and I decided to go the Identification Placement Review Committee (IPRC) route. We were looking for a solution that professionals could give us to help us understand my son's problem. If he was going to have a special placement at school, an IPRC would have to be set up to determine whether he was eligible. This would require different assessments by many specialists. The problem was that it would take time to make appointments with the specialists — the social worker, the psychologist — and to schedule meetings with the homeroom teacher and the special education teacher. These appointments had to be within or after school hours. My husband and I had to accommodate the appointment schedules which meant that one of us had to take time off work. This presented the problem of having to tell our employers and outsiders that we were having a problem with my son.

We loved my son and wanted the best for him. We also adjusted our lives to accommodate his mood of the day or hour. We made short visits to our relatives and having friends over was non-existent. My husband and I traded off personal time — he enjoyed sports, I took a parenting course and went to the occasional fitness class. Things were not easy for my husband and I. I read as much as I could about my son's disability and shared with my husband information that pertained to him as a father. I also tried to keep him updated on strategies that I was trying on my son so that he could be aware of what was happening if asked by a professional. For example, I learned that participation in organized sports would help him increase his social skills and burn off his excess energy. So we enrolled him in T-Ball and his father supported this by becoming his coach. I also found out that children with ADD have trouble switching gears. So I learned some strategies that would redirect a certain behaviour or a train of thought. I also heard a speaker talk about how alone these kids usually feel. If only they could have a friend, a true friend in their lives. This made me grieve. What would happen to him and his care if something happened to his dad and me?

Families tolerate, so did ours. It was draining to educate my son and the rest of the family about his condition, or feel that we had to. Luckily, we had a spacious home and yard. As he grew older, he was able to join us for some activities and play in the back yard. He was able to build constructions from Lego and Construx, and the younger children would admire him for this. But he could also antagonize his siblings if they were showing positive behaviours. For example, when they were playing with friends, he would sabotage their game or interrupt them, or if they were using one of his toys he would demand its return. He could be verbally abusive and this could be embarrassing to everyone. I taught his siblings how they could manage him to the best of their ability, but they knew that they could always come to me if things got out of hand.

He was also very manipulative. He could draw his siblings or daycare children into playing with him because he had good ideas, but then he would become loud and controlling and the children wouldn't want to play with him anymore. He did not have any friends who came over to the house. Other children learned to avoid him.

At eleven or twelve, his hyperactivity slowed down. He tried delivering papers as an age-related responsibility, although he did not do this independently. I did accompany him in inclement weather and helped him with the money collections. My other children could see that I was trying to discipline him or motivate his behaviour. But I was not always successful. Many times his behaviour set the mood in our home. We all learned to get along, to co-exist as best we could.

One weekend in 1992, I was putting laundry away in one of my children's rooms, when my middle son, out of the blue, disclosed to me that my oldest son had been inappropriately touching him and his younger brother. I remember kneeling down to listen, making eye contact with him. What could I say! I felt numb. Luckily, TV programs and the media have informed us of the tragedy of child abuse. So I was knowledgeable enough to tell him that I believed him. Because I did. I had no reason not to. I thought that I could take care of it and that he had done the right thing in telling me.

He ran outside to play. My head was spinning with the words he used, the calmness and suddenness of the disclosure. What now? When will Dad get home? Where was my oldest son now? Then I saw him drive his bicycle into the driveway. He was able to cycle around the block and over to a school playground down the street, which I could see from our front door. Emotionally, I had not yet had time to switch gears and assess how I was feeling. I was still numb from the shock.

Shortly afterwards, my husband returned home from his morning of golf. I took him aside and told him that I had something serious to discuss with him. I was blurting things out to him; he was very shocked. My husband and I took aside our son who had disclosed to me. It was a good opportunity to talk with him: our daughter was at a friend's house, my oldest son was outside riding his bike, and our youngest son was watching TV. My husband wanted to hear from our son what had taken place. My husband and I listened calmly as our son told us, not wanting to put words into the child's mouth. We tried to be delicate. I know this was very awkward for my husband. I at least had some experience with the children's privacy — talking about private areas, helping them in the bathroom, caring for their injuries and sickness. Then we talked with my oldest son who admitted to the accusation against him.

We decided to be as tactful as possible. But my husband and I did not have time to discuss the issue any further at that moment because he was being picked up by his work crew and heading out of town for five days. The next day the kids went to school and I had my usual workload. But the "what nows?" and "what ifs?" started to creep in. Within two days of the disclosure I confided in a friend, or so I thought she was a friend. I was advised by this friend to call the Children's Aid Society (CAS). If I did not, she said she would. Paranoia crept in at this point and has not left since. I felt threatened — this was serious. Should I have told her? I couldn't back out now. Cornered. I felt panic and called my family doctor. She was familiar with our family and the history of my oldest son. I was informed that she would have to report my information. What did that mean? Under the law she was required to do so. The wheels were in motion. I next asked how she could help me. I was referred to Doctor A or Doctor B, pediatricians who dealt with children with ADD. I chose Doctor B who was closer to our family home and would make visits a little easier.

Due to the seriousness of the situation, I was able to make an appointment with Doctor B only twenty-four hours after speaking with my family physician. I went to see him on my own as my husband was still out of town. I told Doctor B my story, as hard as it was to share. I had done nothing wrong. This must have a solution. The legal implications were pointed out. I was scared. I was listening and answering questions as they were asked: from life before I had him, his birth, our marriage, the other siblings, my husband's work, our extended families, school history, work history, "my work."

I told him I took care of other people's children in my home. He asked if there had ever been an opportunity for my son to have been left alone with the other children or if he was ever left in charge temporarily? Was there a possibility? Oh, my god! A light bulb lit up as I grasped the concept of "did he?" and "could he have?" I would have known. But what had actually happened had happened in our own home, when I was just a room away. I had to address this with the doctor and knew in my heart that what had happened to my own children was true. But my son did not have the opportunity to be near enough to the daycare children or be alone with them to have offended them in any way other than verbally. I arranged my daycare hours so that the daycare children would be outside my house when my oldest son came home from school. The parents were also aware of the problem we faced. Each one of my parents had had an opportunity to observe my son's defiant behaviour. Don't get me wrong, my son has many good qualities. But he was disturbed at the time and the behaviours we were dealing with then were peaking. I know this looking back. I always made sure we were outside when most of the daycare kids were picked up and my son was never with us. There was no reason for him to be alone with any of the kids and they didn't care for him much anyway. Some were toddlers and pre-schoolers, a couple were after-school kids. My son kept pretty much to himself, away from the other kids.

But how could I be sure he never got too close? I dissected opportunities. I looked at my calendar, picked out times when maybe he was around them. My husband asked questions to help jog my memory. No, there was never a chance. I will admit, my son could be outspoken and loud when he wanted control of toys that had to be shared. He would tease, use name calling. This only kept the kids away from him. I had enough toys to open a store anyway and had welcoming activities and ongoing transition programs to distract the other children. I liked everyone to be outside for pick ups. This way there was a quick conversation with parents or a daily note in the diaper bag or a craft to make the transition. I feel confident to this day that no daycare child was hurt.

After three hours of history on that first visit, the doctor said he wanted to meet my kids. He also said he would have to report my disclosure. I took all the children the next day after school. I did not tell them where we were going or why. First, I introduced my younger boys to the doctor, who then asked me to leave the room while he talked to them. We waited in the next room; my oldest son, who was then twelve, read magazines. We were the only ones in the doctor's office. Then it was my oldest son's turn. He spoke with the doctor for at least half an hour. Then they were all physically checked. That was a nightmare. I had to get my daughter to undress in front of a man she'd never seen before. After begging and crying, she gave in. It was horrible for them.

When he was finished, the doctor informed me that charges

would probably be laid and that I needed to hire a lawyer for my oldest son. I guess I was in shock and not wanting to show the kids how upset I was — god knows they were already upset enough. So I picked up a pizza and we went home; it was almost seven p.m. My youngest was showing signs of a long day. Me, too! My husband was still out of town. He phoned once or twice to see how we were doing. I updated him on the steps I was taking and he was confident that I would do the right thing. The truth, however, was that I did not know what was going to happen next.

I had to work in the morning. Business as usual. I went through the motions: my own kids to school, my daycare kids arriving and settling in. The next step I was to take had to be the right one. During nap time I called and told the CAS my story and asked what I should do next. We set up a time, and the next day I took the three kids down to the office. My oldest son was in school. During the wait I tried to organize my thoughts. I had had to share so much of our lives personally and openly in the last forty-eight hours. I didn't want to dish out the details of our lives again — I only wanted to reveal what I felt was useful, a condensed version. My memory, thankfully, is vague as to the exact words I used, but my memory of how I felt at the time is still fresh. I asked if I could sit in while my children were being questioned, but I was told that it would be best if I didn't. They stressed that it was important that they talked to the children alone, because I could influence their explained to me how the interview was going to be conducted. I accepted what they said because at the time, I thought they could really help me. I was not aware either that a police officer would sit in on the interview and that it would be recorded.

We went home. I told my oldest son that he would have to go to the CAS for questioning. He was unusually co-operative and went with the flow. Although he knew that he was in trouble, he probably had no idea of what was going to come. We both went to the CAS appointment and my son admitted what he had done. The CAS said there was enough evidence to press charges. I don't recall exactly what happened next, but I think we just went home.

The next day, I received a call and was told that they were definitely going to charge him. I was told to pack my son's clothes. He was to be removed from the home. But where to? I had navigated, advocated for this child for twelve years. How would they know or understand him? The reason, they said, was the safety of the other three. My caring for other children in my home was not central at this time. After school, my son was to be picked up by myself and a plainclothes officer and taken to the police station to be questioned. As luck would have it, I had no daycare children that day. I called my mother-in-law and asked her to pick up my other children at school. An unmarked police car met me and my oldest son in front of the same school. We were taken to police headquarters downtown.

I called a lawyer. She said to work with the police but not to leave my son with them. At the station he was taken into a room and when I tried to follow I was told to sit and wait. I was intimidated and he was interrogated. Charges were laid. I met with a team of social workers who would handle our family's case. Finally, I would get some answers. My son was to be withdrawn from the home and placed in emergency foster care. After his court date, a decision about what was to be done would be made. My husband met me at the police station. At the station, my son was brought before the Justice of the Peace on duty at the time. He examined the charges laid against my son. He told us that the charges were serious enough to go to court and he advised us to retain a lawyer.

The next day, we signed papers putting my son in temporary care for six months.

The social worker assigned to our case was so young, in her early twenties. I found out later that she had no children of her own. Another social worker was assigned to my son. The social workers tried to create an atmosphere of working together to achieve goals. They tried to gain our trust.

I'll never forget the day our social worker came to our home. She came on a Tuesday afternoon. She came to ask me for the names and numbers of all the children that had been under my care and told me not to contact the parents. My reputation was shattered. I could not call them first to prepare them. They trusted and depended on me. Most did not have a back-up sitter. I was terrified of what was to come. I asked what they would be told, but I was put off or asked another question by the social worker.

I was no longer working. Just like death. All relationships ended: my social life, my work, my integrity, my income. The social worker said it was feared my other three would maybe try and abuse the daycare kids. I cried after she left. I was so alone. I wanted to call the parents out of loyalty. To explain. I was to learn all about loyalty.

My husband was out of town on work again. I would have liked to have called him to share the devastating news, but at that time of the day he was still on the job. He phoned me the next night. He could see the position that the CAS had put me in. With my seven years of experience in the childcare business, I could have picked up any odd signs in the children's behaviour. My daycare children had been together since infancy and there was never any unusual behaviours that would have led me to think that there was something wrong with the environment I was providing. I believe that the CAS treated me most unfairly.

The loss of my daycare business was a financial setback, but at the moment, it wasn't a priority. We just wanted to get through each day, walk the kids to school, do the housekeeping chores. We were trying to live a normal life and trying to survive emotionally.

I feel awful for the position I put everyone in. Only when I had more time, months later, did I start to think things over. What had the CAS done for the parents who worked in the morning and expected me to be available? What did the kids feel about being questioned by their own parents? Confusing questions. My home had been a safe, fun place to go each day. I'm sure the families did their best to make other arrangements. A couple called to ask, "Is it true?" Two offered support by not going down to the CAS offices to have their children questioned. They knew their own kids, that we were always outside and that my son was never around the kids. Many other parents never called again. I missed, first of all, their children. But also the friendships I thought we had. The house felt so different with my daycare children and my son gone.

My son had been working towards his Grade Eight graduation. Since being removed from the home and our immediate neighbourhood — the CAS made sure he was as far away as possible — he could not go back to the same school. So I had to go into the school and inform them that he was not coming back. I was given my privacy; no questions were asked. He finished Grade Eight at a Catholic school while in foster care.

I used art as a medium to work with my other kids. It's not easy when you finally have quiet time together to go on, to try and talk about everyday things. Never mind talking to a four-year-old, a seven-year-old and an eight-year-old about what happened. How could I help them? I needed information. Being helpful, how and what was said could be repeated or misinterpreted. My children could see the amount of care that was needed to guide and nurture their oldest brother. I explained to them about foster care and that the people who were taking care of him knew about his problem. Their concern was that all the older daycare children and their parents were aware of the abuse. I reassured them that no details were given out. Up to this day, my children are still concerned about who, other than their grandparents and daycare parents, know about our untold secret. I also reassured them in many ways that, despite the fact that our home life had changed, they had done the right thing in telling me about their brother's behaviour. I also said that we would all work together to make things better. I did not probe the children for any further information about the abuse. I tried to keep home time as normal as possible. The children went from knowing when their oldest brother woke up, what he ate for breakfast, what he wore, what his was mood was to knowing very little about what was going on in his life.

During this time the CAS would call me by phone and let me know what kind of help they were providing my son. They also told me that all the daycare parents had been contacted. I did not know what kind of questions the parents were asked. They also demanded that my other two sons and my daughter attend a program for abused children and suggested that I would benefit from a group for parents who need help in dealing with abuse issues. I was used to being in control, but now I began to feel that the control was out of my hands.

Now I spent my free time, while my kids were in school, finding out information about how this happens and why. Where do we go from here? I spent hours reading medical journals. I spent time in the university library trying to find information about sexual abuse. (Amazingly, there was very little available on the subject at the city libraries.) This was another language — the offender, my kids were victims. My husband and I were, too.

I found it hard to ask at bookstores for specific information. I felt awkward and embarrassed asking for what I needed. One Saturday afternoon I had to get out. I had many times passed the women's bookstore downtown; it had a book I had been looking for. The weather that day was rainy, thundering on and off. Very overcast and gloomy. I got dropped off and needed courage to go in. I liked the atmosphere and the place was small, it appeared empty. I called out so as not to alarm anyone by my presence. I quickly explained that I had called ahead and some books had been put aside for me.

A young woman handed me a pile of books, and I stood there, not knowing where to go and sit so I could read over them. I held them tightly to my chest. Sensing my uneasiness, the young woman suggested that I could sit at the back of the store or go out on the porch. There was a green awning over the porch and a couple of chairs. I curled up with a book and looked around to see if anyone was watching. I skimmed through the books and was not impressed with the information and the statistics before me. I was aware of sex abuse in the news which said that the "offenders" were usually strangers. But what I was beginning to understand was that my son was not a stranger. The feeling of hopelessness and despair for what lay ahead in a world gone crazy overwhelmed me. My world!

Just then the young woman joined me and asked if the books were helpful. Could she assist me more specifically? I was realizing how hard it was to find an exact case scenario for mine, which now had a name: incest. She sat down and helped me gather the books together. I didn't want to go. I loved the rain, and the thunder only punctuated the mood. I was raging with questions, How could this have happened without us seeing? What were the signs? We talked between customers and I was not sure where to go to find more information. She shared a personal story in relation to the topics all discussed in the books. We had a connection. She listened as I shared my frustration with her — is this how it's supposed to go? Am I doing the right thing?

The next hurdle was coping with the CAS. The few meetings we had were usually at our home. Slowly we could feel limits being placed on us. I was never asked about my feelings or the adjustments with my work, or how I was coping. They closed the opportunity to work from my home ever again. How could I give references? Now what would I do? What would I tell others? I felt so alone. Were these the questions to ask our family social worker? When we would connect by phone, I would follow my gut instinct and intuition. The conversation revolved exclusively around the children, there was no room for me to express my feelings, so I did not ask any of these questions. There were times when she seemed to question how I was coping, because I appeared calm and not angry at my oldest son.

We were uneducated in the ways of the law, of lawyers, counsellors, group homes, probation and its terms. We were in a whirlpool of a new world that had suddenly taken over our lives.

Our family social worker called and informed us that a course was beginning that dealt with the family and that offered my husband and me a supportive place to talk to other parents in similar situations. The children would be in age-appropriate groups with leaders. We were strongly encouraged to attend: for seven weeks. I enrolled the family and we had our introductory meeting with the program co-ordinator. Finally, I might find some support and have some questions answered. My husband decided not to attend. He did support us by taking us and picking us up.

The family groups had been operating on a regular basis for I don't know how long. Each group had two to three leaders, plus ten to twenty kids in each group. Nervously, my children and I went to our groups and tried to participate. Our attendance was checked and a report sent to the CAS. We spent seven weeks doing this. The children knew that they were required to attend. They met some other kids they could relate to and enjoyed doing the craft activities. These activities were supposed to help them get their feelings out. They were also taught about their rights to their own bodies. The groups I attended, however, were not at all helpful to me. On the contrary, I brought information to share with the groups.

My oldest son was also required to take a course called an "offenders group" run by the CAS to help him deal with his offence, with power and control issues, and to come to terms with the fact that he was at fault and that the others were not. They also talked to him about methods that he could fall back on so that he would not offend again.

Then we had the court hearings. Thirteen charges were laid against my son. They itemized every little infraction, for example, sexual touching, threatening, confinement. Things were not settled in the first court appearance. It took four appearances and visits to lawyers in between. My husband had to take time off work as it appeared more supportive with the two of us in attendance. It was always asked and noted who was there to support the offender. As the hearings were in progress, my son moved from a foster home to a group home, where he had to adjust to new rules and where they had behaviour modification programs. These changes were hard on him, so his negative behaviour escalated. He became aggressive to other kids in the group home. During the court sessions, however, he did as he was told. He sat with his lawyer and answered when he was spoken to. Finally, the judge ordered a psychological assessment and the hearings were adjourned for a few weeks.

My son was placed in a group home and put on probation. It was not easy for him because the CAS had to consider two things: that he would receive appropriate care and that he would not offend other children. Of course he was being counselled and a social worker was assigned to him. She or he would tell us how the group home operated and how my son was fitting in.

Soon afterwards, the relationship between the CAS and our family took a drastic turn for the worse. One day, while I was out running errands, the social worker arrived at my kids' school and wanted to talk to them. Only two were there as afternoon classes had not started yet. I had told my children that if the CAS ever came to their school to question them, that they were to call me, because I wanted to be present. My oldest son had made allegations that I had pulled his sister's hair and lifted her off the ground by her pony tail. The social worker wanted to speak to her to see if this was true. My daughter was called to the office. She was scared, asked if she could use the bathroom and ran upstairs to her French teacher's classroom. While she was running down the hallway, she passed her brother (my middle son) who was also coming to the office to be questioned. The French teacher comforted her. The CAS came to the classroom to try to remove my daughter, but the teacher did not allow it. At this point, my son was down in the office; he was very upset at having seen his sister so distraught. He asked the secretary to call me. Since I wasn't home, the secretary called my mother-in-law, who was at work. She came to the school immediately and picked up my son and daughter.

In the meantime, I was coming to the school from downtown with my youngest son to drop him off for his afternoon class. My mother-in-law drove to our home, but I wasn't there. My son and daughter must of told her that I was planning on dropping off their brother, so she returned to the school and parked the car nearby, waiting for me. When the children saw me, they came out of the car and ran to me; they looked scared and were rambling. My mother-in-law filled me in on what had taken place. I took the kids home and asked my neighbours to mind them while my mother-in-law and I went back to the school to find out more. We spoke to the principal, who informed us that the CAS had requested to speak to my children and the school was obligated by law to comply. Later that day, the CAS worker phoned me at home and asked why the children had acted the way they did. By then I had developed an attitude and explained to her that I had told my children that they were not to be questioned without me present. Naturally, the social worker was not happy about this and let me know it.

The experience at school did not go well for anyone. How dare they?! The CAS did this without my knowledge or permission. Our feelings were further trampled on, however, when we found out that they could question our kids in their office or at our home, but we would need to be out of the room. Then a day or two later, my husband and I were served an affidavit. The allegations in it questioned our parenting methods. The CAS was asking the courts to give them one hundred percent care of our oldest son. They would make all the decisions, and we would be advised accordingly.

When something is wrong, I try to make it right. We decided to stand up for ourselves. We needed an advocate, someone to help us get along with *those* who were *supposed to be* helping us in the first place. We are well-educated people, yet we felt helpless, losing control of one child. We felt we had been judged by these people, our social worker, the very people we turned to for help. They were questioning our parenting skills and making written insinuations against our position as parents.

I called the Children's Advocacy and was put through to a representative. A meeting was arranged at our home. She was very professional and did not take sides. She asked questions. She outlined where she could help. We worked together with her, although my husband and I made all final decisions.

We hired a lawyer to defend us in these allegations, and we did clear our name and reputation, but at a cost. It took several years for us to repay our legal debts. All trust in the CAS and their methods has been destroyed. They have too much power and when they want to wield it, they do. We had to prove our innocence to them. They overreacted to comments made from a young man who was confused and who may have been manipulated. We were not there to hear and react for ourselves. The price of that was heavy for us all. The CAS also have at their fingertips a legal department. So, when they require assistance, it's not affecting them personally or financially.

Once my oldest son turned eighteen years old, his probation ended. Consequently, he has taken control of his treatment and can make decisions about his own living arrangements. He moved out of the group home and now lives independently and works for a construction company. He still has poor decision-making skills; for a time he had a substance abuse problem, due to mixing alcohol with his antidepressant. To my knowledge, he still doesn't have any friends. His only interaction with peers is through work.

As for my other children, two are now in high school and they seem to have put what happened behind them. My oldest son has spent time in our home and the other children seem comfortable with the idea, although they are cautious with him. I feel that it is important that the mistakes he made in his life are used as a teaching tool.

It took a couple of years for me to find a new job, and slowly I'm getting my life back on track. I feel like I have helped everybody heal and move on, now it is my turn to heal my inner wounds. My husband and I got through this together, and we now feel that we have the same challenges as most parents do.

Mothering: Is This A Job Or ...?

TONI SANO

I've done several different kinds of work. I have a university degree in applied mathematics and computer science. I worked in a large company for a couple of years as a computer programer. Subsequently, I worked for three different companies, ending up as a systems analyst at a very traditional male-oriented manufacturing company. I was the first woman hired in my department and it was quite an interesting experience. At one of the other places I worked, which was unionized, I lost out on a job opportunity; somebody else who had less experience received a promotion because he wasn't making as much money as his wife and this was upsetting him.

Since about 1989 I have been at home. When we adopted our third child, I took a maternity leave. I had hoped to return to work part-time, as I did with the first two when they were small, but a change in management denied me that option. So with my husband working full-time, we decided that I would become a full-time parent. We then had three children under seven. My eldest child has just become a teenager. All my children have special needs of one kind or another. So I now think of myself as a professional mother and that is, I find, a very full-time job.

The work of mothering has affected my health. I'm in very good health normally. I have the usual number of colds. I have no major illnesses, nothing like that. But I had a nervous breakdown and became clinically depressed. I don't think the breakdown was caused by any one thing. I think it was the result of many years of stress and of advocating in particular for my one child who has considerable difficulties both socially and in school. The nervous breakdown was the result of the proverbial straw that breaks the camel's back. I had been going full-tilt, budgeting the household finances and coming to terms with how much money we had, and coming to terms with my children's disabilities and their different needs. It's very hard to accept that your children are not who you thought they were going to be, and it's also hard for the children when they have to realize that they're not what they thought they were going to be.

Adoption is a very different way to have a family. When we got married we knew that my husband was unable to have children. We went to an infertility clinic and for about a year we did try the donor insemination program. That was an interesting experience because you have to fork out twenty-five bucks a time for the semen. It's probably more now. There was some matching done between my husband's characteristics and the donor's characteristics. But now that I have adopted children and I have a lot of information about their backgrounds I wonder, would I tell a child who is the product of artificial insemination about their medical background, and how important would that be? I think not telling is a way to hide the reality of the child's background. I think if I had to do it now and I had a child by donor insemination, I would at some point tell the child that.

Anyway, artificial insemination didn't work for us and we decided to adopt. We began the adoption process by submitting our names to the local Children's Aid Society. After a two-year wait, we were contacted by a social worker for a "home study," or *their* study of *us*. We had several interviews with the social worker, provided personal and bank references and our life histories, and shared our views on parenting and our coming to terms with infertility. Once our home study was approved by the CAS, it was only a matter of time before we received a child. Each subsequent adoption required a separate home study. As a parent who has had to have a seal of approval, as I call it, placed on her home study, I find it very frustrating to hear stories of mothers and parents who don't necessarily have the abilities required to parent a child and who don't pass the test. For us, we had to be ready; we did a lot of hard thinking and had to come to terms with many adoption issues.

Our first child arrived in mid 1981 and our second in late 1982. Our third child arrived in the fall of 1988 and our fourth in early 1990. All of them were infants or toddlers when they came to us. One of the children has a visible physical disability. The other children, we eventually discovered, have either learning disabilities or Attention Deficit Disorder (ADD). Many children who are adopted have special needs of one type or another and that's okay, we're quite happy to have adopted children who have special needs. What has been hard is that we didn't anticipate these needs.

We know a bit about their personal histories. We know all of them were born in Ontario, but only our first child has a European background. The other three have mixed heritages that include Asian, Native, Filipino and European. We don't know much about their parents. Two of our children came to us from foster homes and for them this was a traumatic experience. They experienced separation anxiety and fear of their new living situation. Our child with the physical disability needs several visits a year to a clinic for physiotherapy and occupational therapy. She also needs modifications at school to enable her to sit at her desk and participate in gym. Our son with the hardest needs is also the child with the least visible needs. He suffers from ADD, which is a frustrating disability for him, his siblings, his parents and those who meet him. His early school years were a nightmare because he couldn't do his tasks, follow instructions or line up for recess. He often acted out and was a real challenge for his teachers. At home, we had to constantly keep an eye on him. We couldn't leave him alone for a minute. Even taking a moment to go to the bathroom was impossible until he was asleep.

We've been very open with our children about their biological backgrounds and about the circumstances around their adoption. We have told them most of what we know about how we adopted them. We have photos of our first meeting with each of them. They know their biological parents chose adoption. I have shown one of them the maternity home where the biological mother spent her pregnancy. Another knows that there is an older sibling adopted by another family. One of my children knows the name of his mother because she told him, she has written it down for him. At one point one of my children was going through a hard stage and chose to send a Valentine to her birth mother. She was making Valentine's cards for me and my husband in school and made one for her birth mother and mailed it off.

I'm hoping that our acceptance of their adoption and their original families will go a long way towards making them comfortable with their adoption. I've read a lot about adoption and I really believe adoption is an issue which never ever goes away. It's like being very freckled or something, and people always notice that, or you're always aware that you're just a little different. It's not a bad kind of different, it's just a difference. For instance, I often go to the supermarket with one of my children to do the shopping. If I leave my child in the buggy and walk a little bit away from the buggy, but am still able to see my child and am close enough to be the obvious parent, people will look around and say, "Oh there's an unattended child." In fact, I am attending to my child but nobody would connect me automatically with my younger children because they are of a different racial heritage.

When you have a biological child you and others can usually see characteristics of yourself in your child and you can, sort of, often understand where your child is coming from. That's one of the issues with adoption. You may not know where a trait is coming from. For example, your child can be very temperamentally different and you have no basis for comparison; it's just that you don't have any previous experience with that kind of temperament. That's been an issue for me, and certainly for me and my son who is very different and has very different behaviours related to his disability.

It's been a real challenge learning to meet his needs. He's in a very specialized school program, which has been very good for him. The staff has been trained. His behaviours are such that on occasions he has to be restrained which means that someone has to physically put him down on the floor and hold him until he's back in control of himself. This was completely unlike anything that I had ever experienced in my life. I consider myself a good parent. I consider myself a well-educated parent. But the kind of parenting he needs is very, very specialized and it's taken a long time to learn. I'm still learning and I will probably always need to learn how to meet his needs.

For example, I need to carefully plan before I take him shopping. I talk to him about acceptable behaviour at the grocery store and let him know that if he behaves properly he'll receive a treat at the end of the shopping. But I have also learned to be ready to abandon the shopping trip altogether if he gets out of control (running away from me, throwing canned goods). Some days I can judge that this is a bad day to take him shopping and I make alternative plans. Other family expectations have also had to change. For example, I can only plan very short visits to family or friends. Learning things like positive or negative consequences, providing a lot of nurturing and a home where he is safe takes a lot of work. Until he was in his teens, if he was outside playing, I would be out there with him supervising him and ready to intervene if he became aggressive.

I've been seeing a therapist for about three years to help me cope with my children's disabilities. To cope with them I've had to come to terms with myself and with my low self-esteem. I'm a very fortunate woman. I was not abused as a child but I did grow up with very low self-esteem. I grew up as a very shy person and some of my coping mechanisms I learned as a child have helped me to keep going no matter what. But in the last year, we have gone through some traumatic times with my oldest child. We had voluntarily placed him in foster care for eighteen months, which was done through child welfare and family court. Foster care was good for all of us and the foster parents were wonderful people. But child welfare and the court agreed not to have any further involvement with our family and my son came home. After the final meeting with them, I came home and went to bed — for about a week. This is totally unlike me, I normally cope with everything. I closed the bedroom door and I said to my husband, "You do everything." I didn't do housework, I didn't get the children off to school, I didn't cook, I didn't do laundry, I didn't do anything. I actually have very little memory of this time.

After a week or so I went to my therapist. I was ninety-nine percent sure that I was clinically depressed. My therapist and I reviewed the symptoms of depression. My major ones were total exhaustion and being very irritable to the extent that I could not handle being around the children at all. I was also so exhausted that I didn't get out of bed. He agreed that I was depressed and I started on a low dose of medication. The medication is similar to Prozac. (It's not Prozac. I consider myself a well-educated lay person. I had read books about Prozac before he put me on it. I went to the library and researched the side effects.)

One of the problems with this kind of medication is that it takes about a month before you can tell whether it's effective. I started at a low dose, but after about four weeks we increased the dosage. Now it's at a dosage that seems to be therapeutic and I am functioning somewhat. I am able to get through the day. I still don't get the children off to school, so my husband has really had to do his part. It's been really good for him. It has really helped his self-esteem, to take over and do that. It did mean that he had to take a leave of absence from his job because I was just too sick to do anything. And as a result of being so depressed I have learned that I have to take better care of myself and I am now better able to recognize when I am feeling tired, when I'm feeling uptight, when I'm feeling anxious, and I stop what I'm doing and leave the room. I also find that, although I think I'm feeling well, if I do too much then I pay for it the next day and I spend the next couple of days in bed.

My depression has been an interesting experience for my children. I haven't been totally up-front with them. All I've said is that I've been very tired, that I got sick, and that it's going to take me a long time to get well and that I'm taking medication. Now I think the older one has heard that it's a nervous breakdown and I haven't really gone through that with him. I will have to explain it to them in more detail. It's been hard for my immediate family, too. When I first mentioned it to some of my family, they said, "Oh there's this virus going around. Don't worry, you'll be better soon." It wasn't until I'd said it a couple of times that my family made some kind of acknowledgement that this was indeed depression. At first I didn't tell my friends and acquaintances and the volunteers I associate with.Then as time went on I told a few people. Generally, I have very sane and sensible friends, and they understood that depression is a medical illness and that part of it is caused either by a lack of neuro-transmitters or by neuro-transmitters not working the way they normally do. They see it as an illness, just like diabetes. For diabetes you use insulin, for depression you take seratonin thingamajiggys. And that's okay.

I've been quite encouraged by the responses I've received from people. I feel quite comfortable that it's an illness, that it's treatable — the two treatments being medication and talking therapy. I'm doing my best with both of these. I believe that eventually I will be back to where I was and doing all that I was doing, although maybe I was doing too much. I was fighting on all fronts and I was going non-stop. When I am well, I will be going at a slower pace, a more reasonable pace and a more accepting pace of what I can and cannot do.

Learning to do work at a more comfortable pace means learning to set limits, both in terms of the children's demands on me and in terms of the volunteer demands on me. Like many women, I was socialized to be a caregiver, to be nurturing, to do as much as I could to assist others, and in the process I lost me. Take my volunteer work, for example. I love my volunteer work. I have gained so much from it. I have met so many people. I have done so much networking. I've benefited. I've grown. I've been educated in many different fields. But I sometimes feel that some of the volunteer organizations — for instance Meals on Wheels or hospital auxiliaries — take advantage of women's good nature and their unpaid work. It's as if women's volunteer work is a way for society to get something for nothing. I wouldn't want to ever criticize a woman who chooses to volunteer, but I sometimes find that women's volunteer time is work they are never paid for, and this just continues the lack of respect for the value of women's traditional unpaid work.

Mothering is another form of unpaid work. On top of housework, there's the work of nurturing and meeting everyone else's needs except your own. The mother is the CEO (chief executive officer) of the family. It's been partly because of the children's needs that I've gone overboard, trying to make sure that their needs are met. It's a very fine line between meeting their needs and giving them everything — what we used to call spoiling. Setting limits means you have to be brave enough to risk that someone may not like you for what you do. That has been a real issue for me, accepting that not everybody will like me and that it's in my children's best interests for me to say no and to have them say they don't like it and to cope with their anger. Anger is another part of it, too. I don't know if it's true for all women, but it's true for me — I'm very uncomfortable around angry people and I will do a lot to keep the peace. And that's not done my kids any favours. In therapy I have been working through these issues and learning that it's okay to set limits, that it's okay for children to be angry, that it's okay for me to be angry. Learning how to mother differently isn't easy, but it's helping me learn how to take care of me, too.

Coping with my depression is very much like coping with a disability. The experience has given me a deeper appreciation for my children's situations. A close family member has an artificial limb and is regarded by society as being disabled. Our family sees her as a person who has a disability. She receives incredible sympathy and support, both financial and in terms of accommodation. Yet for mental or neurological or cognitive disabilities, that level of support and understanding just isn't there. I guess one of my crusades in life is to help the big world out there understand that the invisible disabilities can be as equally severe as the visible physical ones. I think my mental illness has also helped me come to terms with the fact that disabilities cover such a broad range of things and that everybody is unique.

One of the things I talk a lot to my children about is that being different is okay. I think our society places a tremendous value on not being different. We all know about teenagers and peer pressure, but it starts very young. In terms of disabilities, it's part of the same issue: it's okay to be different, it's okay to be visibly different, it's okay to learn differently. I have this anecdote about how important our society considers it that none of us be different: when there's a newborn child, and the newborn child is a boy and the parents are making the decision as to whether or not to circumcise the child, the issue comes down to should he be the same as Daddy? If we can't accept that father and son can be different, we're in big trouble as a society in terms of accepting women, in terms of accepting visible minorities, in terms of accepting people with disabilities.

Society doesn't recognize a disabled child's needs or the needs of families with disabled children. This doesn't make it any easier. Every family is unique and has individual strengths and needs. The needs of any one family often do not match the social services available. Often, families don't know that there are services available. The services also vary from region to region and may depend on the diagnosis or the perceived severity of the disability. It often seems as if children with disabilities are regarded as a drain on society and seen as charitable cases. As a consumer of services for children with disabilities, the frustration I go through in terms of accessing services, in accessing funds, is incredible. Having to describe in very negative terms my child's needs is incredibly depressing because although he's very needy, he also has incredible strength. He can be an absolute delight!

We are on family benefits. It's a depressing place to be. If you haven't been there, you have no idea. You are only allowed to have very limited amount of assets which means that you cannot, for instance, save up for a vacation because if you have savings then you have assets and you're not eligible for benefits. Or if you have Registered Retirement Savings Plans, they are considered assets and you have to cash them in. We've gone from living a middle-class life style on a middle-class income to trying to live a middle-class life style on an income lower than the poverty line. What really hurts is that we can't give the children what they want. I have worked very hard to find things that we can afford, but it's not always possible to provide my children with what they need or would like. For instance, one of my children would really benefit from some of the community recreation programs. But I'm not sure where the money is going to come from to pay for him to continue in those programs. The budgeting goes on endlessly. I'm always saying, "Well, I'll pay this creditor this month and that creditor next month." We were actually doing okay until I had my breakdown and then I wasn't on top of it. Now I'm thinking,

"Oh, my God, where do I go from here?" I'm just going to have to keep on plugging away and watching every penny. It really affects the children when I say, "Well, we can't buy you the kinds of Christmas presents or the kinds of birthday presents that we'd like to buy you." Or, when there's a school trip— especially the end-of-the-year trips in June — and it costs money, and the kids want a couple of bucks for spending, which they can't have. If I do give them money, then it means, well, there just won't be as much money for groceries that week.

One of the things I've started to do is use the food banks. And that's depressing. I am grateful to society for providing food banks. I am also angry. We have children with needs. I have my depression and my husband had to take an early retirement due to health reasons. All of this makes it very hard for us to work and make an income that would support a family with four children, all of whom have disabilities. Even when using food banks is taken into account, there still isn't enough money. Then I read about more cutbacks and that's very scary. And when I read that we have universal healthcare, I think, "Well, we have universal healthcare but it doesn't pay for non-prescription drugs. It doesn't pay for the fact that if I want two hours of peace the only way I'm going to get it is to rent a movie because that will keep my son occupied." Is that healthcare? I'm not sure, but if I don't meet my needs then I don't meet his needs. There are times when, if it's four dollars to rent two movies, I will do it even though I know that we really can't afford it. Living on a poverty level income means you spend your life making choices, but not the choice of where shall we have a vacation or where shall we eat out this week? It's the choice between shall I pay the bills or shall I buy summer clothing for my children? My two youngest are getting older and they're not very happy with Bi-way, so what can I do? I can go to other places where you can buy clothing very cheap, and that's probably what I'm going to have to do.

It's really hard on the children. I don't mind living on a poverty-level income. I don't mind that I can't afford a case of beer. I'm not a big drinker anyway. I don't mind it. I've cut back all the optional spending. I don't mind that I had to wait and wait and wait before I bought myself a pair of shoes because my kids needed shoes more than I did. It's the stress related to living in poverty that makes it so hard. Does society have an obligation to support us? Society says it will look after those who are less fortunate, but that's done in a very begrudging fashion. I would like to be a contributing member. I think I am. I think I am raising my children to the best of my ability and doing a really good job, but given my children's disabilities I can't go out and work full-time. They require full-time care. I can't expect my husband to go out to work because he's sick, too, and he's helping to care for our family. It's a very two-faced society. We say children are important. We say family is important. We say that we need to raise our children. I read about young offenders, I read about violence in society and what it all boils down to is that we need to give our children the best. If we don't give our children the best now, we will pay infinitely more, both financially and as a society, to meet these children's needs in the future.

No description of my life would be complete without mentioning my faith in God. I was born and raised a Catholic and I'm still a Catholic. I consider myself a feminist Catholic, or a Catholic feminist. I have considerable disagreements with the Church in several areas, like many women. On the other hand I figure if it took them four hundred years to acknowledge that Galileo was right, eventually they'll agree that I'm right — as are so many others — that it's okay for women to be priests and it's okay for priests to marry. I think it's very sad that the Church is not comfortable with that. I hope eventually they realize that women have a great deal to contribute and would make excellent priests and could do everything that male priests can do. I also go to Church most Sundays and I find that that's the one hour a week I look at the big picture instead of the little picture. The big picture is that God is in my life and it takes me out from being self-centred and just concentrating on my concerns. I still have trouble with why God chose my children to have disabilities, especially the one whose disability is really hard on him and really hard on us. I read a really good book called *Why Do Bad Things Happen To Good People?* by Rabbi Kushner. That helped. On my good days, when I'm saying, "Why me God, why me? Why him, why him?" I turn it around and say, "Why not me, why not him?" If a child was going to be born with this disability, there was a reason God chose this child to be our child.

As for me, when I look at the issue of how to improve my depression, one of the things I need to do is work out my relationship with God. Often I revisit the question, Why me, why him? I have to go through being really angry with God because my son is tormented, my son has times when he says, "I don't want to live." That is really hard for a kid and it's very hard for a parent to know her kid feels like that. There are times when his life is so hard that that is a very realistic question for him.

I'm very comfortable with the idea of an image of God as feminine. To me God is just as much feminine as masculine. I am happy to think of God as a Goddess, as a mother image. Some of this imagery is in the Bible if you know where to look. It's just that most of the Bible was written for a patriarchal society, and we're stuck with it. I'm interested in the religions which are Goddess based — Wicca and so on. I don't know a lot about them but I find them very accepting. Whereas originally it was always He that was used to refer to God, we're now beginning to see She. Saying She expands the mental images I have of God. I can expand the concept of God as archetypical "father" — the boss, the wage earner, disciplinarian — to "mother" — the nurturer, friend.

Material Things That Bite

D. LUSSIER NANSON

In my early years I remember smiling and laughing like a carefree child visiting my grandmother, laughing with siblings, learning about my heritage or the good part of it. Then one day it all changed to become worse than a child could ever imagine.

If only it were a dream, but this is a part of my life as I lived it. I do not remember ever going hungry or wearing dirty clothes, but I vividly remember the beatings. I remember being chased by a white station wagon driven by my father across the school yard of Falls View school. As I ran, I cried and screamed for my mother and tried to climb the fence in our back yard for safety, until he came around the block and into the driveway.

Another time I remember all of us getting spanked because my youngest sister made a call to California, for this my mother also got a few slaps.

I remember having a pink easy-bake oven and getting a beating for taking a light bulb out of my room to make it operate. I remember being handcuffed to the front door by a friend of the family because I said I wanted to run away from home and live with my grandmother.

Going to my grandmother's was so peaceful. I remember going across the street from my grandmother's to gaze at the Niagara River — so peaceful. Grandfather told me to respect this lady called Niagara as she could take your life. Yet look at the beauty she holds. I used to swing my grandmother's Siamese cat Lynx by the tail in circles until I heard my grandmother coming, then I would let him go. He would retreat to a window ledge, glaring at me with blue-green eyes of hate. I despised this creature because he was allowed to live with my grandmother and I was not, and I felt so utterly alone when I had to return home.

Once, upon arriving home from my grandmother's, I found out that we were moving to a farm — something we had wanted to do, or so we thought. What do children know? We were about to pay for that farm with our bodies, sweat and tears. We were given to by one hand while beaten with the other. Oh, I learned that material things can bite. I remember as if it were only a moment ago, being beaten in the barn for not clearing the stalls properly with the electric manure mover. I was dumbfounded. My black German Shepherd named Duke was chained in the barn, and he began growling when my father started beating me, lunging at him. I was beaten all the way down to the house. In the morning when I awoke, Duke was gone.

Dead? Who knows? I was told he ran away. How could he, from inside a locked barn?

Welcome to farm life, Deborah. Our farm had a red brick house, two barns and a pond by the road. There was a country club up the road and a few neighbours. Slowly, my father purchased animals. We were to each receive a horse of our own, but not without paying for it, believe me. We had horses, a cow named Daisy, a goat my mother named Gregory, a rooster and geese that turned out to be my enemies. I used to tease them until one day they cornered me coming up the driveway, flapping their wings as they ran towards me. I screamed and screamed and didn't escape without bruises, learning they are not docile creatures.

Mornings were fun, but in the winter it was cold, farm-country cold. I remember the Blizzard of '77, blankets of snow, the house was covered. Father had to shovel his way to the barn to save the animals. Now I find that strange in some ways, as he beat them just like he beat us.

My uncle John stopped visiting because of the way my father treated us children. Soon hardly anybody visited 9858 Nichols Lane.

Arc of My Life

D. LUSSIER NANSON

The arc of the horseshoe as the water
thunders over
Rock hits water, bruises under
clothes
Grandfather, from you I take some
entitlements of my life as you've
conquered Niagara
  sincerity
  heart
  the art of conquering
Grandmother, from you I learned
  to love
  to assist
  to smile from my heart
Mother, from you I learned to deny
all that was happening to me or
  to minimize
Father Uncle Abuser
  I learned to
hate
rebel
and hurt
All I have learned and yet I know
not who I am.

I Wish

TRACY FRANKLIN

To K and E

I would love to be more the one
that my child ever needs

Society in its wisdom though
has planted its own seeds

The work day begins long
before my child wakes
And ends when I'm so tired
energy cannot be faked

It's been this way for a long time
so that a life for her could be made

Along the way she grew up on me
I'm scared our few
shared memories together will fade

I know she knows I love her though
I can see it in her eyes

Yet in a short time
she'll move on from me and
there will have to be goodbyes

In time I hope she understands
I did the best I could
I provided in the necessary ways
so there was not much time for fun

Oh my wonderful child
I wish I could be more the one

My Story

CAROL HENHAWK

My mother already had a child when she had me; she was young. Her mom, my grandmother, grew up in the mushhole (residential schools) and she was very strict. She could speak three Iroquois dialects but she wouldn't speak Iroquois when she got home because my grandfather would beat her or because he thought she was talking about him. He only spoke English. So my mother grew up in family violence. I think she was maybe eighteen when she was pregnant with me; she couldn't handle another screaming baby. I couldn't wait to come out into the world; we were driving down the road to the hospital in Ohsweken and I popped out.

My mother tells me that my birth was a horrible experience because of what happened to her when she got to Lady Wellington Hospital. There was no respect for her as a person, they didn't wash her up for a day or so; it was just a horrible experience. I guess her way of wiping that out was to give me away to my aunt Rainey and uncle Bob. They had been looking for a child, because my aunt couldn't have any. She had had three or four pregnancies and had lost them; she couldn't carry them full term. My uncle was often drunk and he was very abusive to my aunt, but they thought that bringing me into the home would change that. So they did, they took me in and they gave me a lot of love.

When I was about two, this uncle — whom I call my father — fell down some stairs. He was drunk and it was wet outside. He broke something in his spine and became a paraplegic. My aunt was very committed. After all the abuse — she once said there wasn't a place on her body that wasn't bruised — she could have just walked away and left him. I can imagine what kind of abuse she had to go through. We were very isolated, my uncle Bob was in and out of hospital, in traction. He'd get fluid on his lungs, so there were times when I was left with my other aunt and uncle, Jane and Rick, for long periods. It was there where the sexual abuse began, and that was on the reserve.

I had thirteen cousins there, one of whom was younger than me and all the rest were older. There were two girls, and all the rest were boys. They were sexually abusive with one another and with me, not physically abusive — even with my aunt Jane at home. She had arthritis, so she couldn't get up and around. She couldn't do anything to stop it, even if she had wanted to. Uncle Rick was sexually abusive, too. I don't remember too much about that. I am working on remembering those times, but I know there was a lot of pain, a lot of humiliation as a child and it showed up when I became a teenager. All those times being alone with them, I remember running and hiding and sitting in a corner crying, many times, not sure why I was crying, but I remember there was a lot of pain.

After a period of my uncle Bob being in and out of the hospital — that was before I turned five — he ended up in Sunnybrook Hospital in Toronto. They thought there was a chance that he might walk. That was a really beautiful place to be as a child, because for once in my life I felt needed. The hospital was a safe place; it was safe from abuse. When we lived in Toronto and I'd spend a lot of time at Sunnybrook, I saw a lot of pain — physical pain, emotional pain, spiritual pain caused by losing limbs, losing the ability to function as a normal person, even to get up and get your own drink of water. I spent a lot of time with other patients, and when I'd walk in I'd be their "sunshine." I'd be this little girl running around, asking, "Do you need a drink of water? Do you want this, do you want that?" I'd push them in a wheelchair down to the activity room and, they'd say, "Well, hold me," because it was a ramp and I was just a little girl, but the nurse was always behind me. I just felt so loved. I don't remember being too much with my uncle Bob.

Me and my aunt Rainey, we lived in Toronto for two years, alone in an apartment. That was really rough, not having uncle Bob there, not having any other children to be around. I started kindergarten there, and my aunt said I used to "play hooky" all the time. That was because I was so scared of other kids and I didn't know how to get along. We moved after two years, when they found that my uncle Bob couldn't or didn't want to walk. I chose to believe that he couldn't, but in my heart I know that he could have, if he'd wanted to. He had gotten into a lot of medication by then and abused the medication, and he started drinking again when we got home. It was back to the same old thing, but I think it got worse when we got home. I must have been about six or seven when we got back to the reserve from Toronto.

I went to school off reserve since we lived so close to the borderline. My uncle Bob was a franchised Indian, so we lived on the edge of Heaven with all the other franchised Indians and with the halves who had lost their status through marriage. At that point I had seen my uncle Bob abuse himself by taking the drugs and taking the alcohol and it hurt me, yet I felt I had to take care of his emotional state. He was a very depressed man, and cried a lot. He made comments like "I'm not good enough, I might as well be dead." I used to go out and get him flowers, try to do something with him. I remember sitting on the edge of his bed or getting him to cuddle me. I always admired him and he made me very angry because he could have walked, he could have, it was like he betrayed me. I thought, "You must not love me enough to take care of yourself, to get yourself together."

When we got home and I had to spend time at my aunt Jane and uncle Rick's house, the abuse began again, with my uncle and cousins. I did my best to please them. It had gotten to the point where I think I had bought into the idea that this was my mission in life, this was how you pleased people, because I always felt so empty. I was so young, yet I was trying to act like an adult woman, you know? I was thinking that I was an adult woman having to fulfill sexual relationships when it was demanded of me. My cousins had trained me to do that.

At least I had one safe place and that was at my uncle Bob and aunt Rainey's home, but my uncle Bob's drinking had gotten worse. Something that was really odd, that used to bother me, was that when I was a kid, I had to play outside, 'cause my aunt would say, "Get outside, Uncle's drunk again." We had a small house and my uncle's bed was in the main room, which was our kitchen. Sitting outside I would think, "Well, Uncle can't walk, but still he gets drunk, where's he getting the alcohol from?" I didn't understand my aunt Rainey. I saw her as a strong person who washed him, cleaned his sheets every day, cleaned the house, made the supper. She was always very dependable — she knew what she had to do and she did it, she didn't think about it, she just did it. But the thing I couldn't understand was, why was she so dependent?

My uncle couldn't walk, all she would have had to do was say, "I don't want to take you to buy booze." But I can remember driving around this reserve, and I knew every bootlegger on the reserve and off.

Many older men came to our house, drunk. I would be so angry because it was my aunt's fault, it was my uncle's fault, I didn't know whose fault. "Why are you doing this to me, why do I have to go hide, why do I always have to be around adults, why can't I play with other kids?" My friends were always scared. My aunt Rainey was always scared of me getting abused or hurt by the men at the house, but I couldn't tell her what was happening at my uncle Rick's house. And the men who came to the house would say — I don't know, I don't know how to explain it — they'd say, "Oh, hello little girl." You could just smell the booze on them and they'd be peeing their pants and saying, "Come here and give me a big hug and kiss." And that's what I grew up with.

So I started going into a fantasy world and that was the TV. I had ideas of what I would be like as an adult and I already thought that I was an adult in every way, because I had to be dependable, I had to be. Plus I was having this sexual life. I had bought into the fact that that's what I was there for. TV was my world. I can name any actor or actress from TV shows even today. TV brought me up, that was my entertainment, that's all I had.

There were kids next to us, kids on the other side, kids behind us, but I was never allowed to play with them, because on this side there was something wrong with them, on that side there was something wrong with that family. My aunt Rainey kept me very isolated.

The clearest memory of sexual abuse that I have happened when I was older, and I think at that time I came to a turning point. I must have been about eight or nine. One of my cousins, who was one of my abusers, had stayed at my aunt and uncle's house and of course he just kept on abusing me there. I think I had come to a point where I didn't want that anymore, I realized something was wrong. I think that was the first time that I felt that something was wrong. I said to myself, "I don't want this anymore, I don't like this. There must be something wrong with this."

It wasn't much longer after that my uncle Bob died. I came home from school one day and aunt Rainey and uncle Bob weren't home. I stayed outside and waited and then they pulled up in a taxi. My aunt had this big white bandage around her chest. They had been in a car accident. My uncle looked fine and my aunt took him in, got him all cleaned up and put him to bed. But I knew something was wrong. I remember waking up the next morning and his bed was gone. I remember wondering what my other aunts and uncles were doing there. One of my uncles took me to my aunt's side and said, "Your uncle Bob's gone, he's in a better place." I was thinking, "Oh yeah, he's gone to the hospital." I just couldn't fathom the idea "gone, what's gone, is he dead?" I didn't know how to talk about that. I think I knew what "dead" was, 'cause I had a bird that died and it just wouldn't move after that, so I knew what "dead" meant, but I didn't understand what he was telling me. I thought he was playing games with me.

I ended up over at my cousins' again. I don't remember what happened to my aunt Rainey, she just sort of faded off. I think she had a lot of broken bones from the car accident, but we hadn't talked and I ended up back in my abusive aunt and uncle's house while Aunt Rainey took care of the funeral. I was driving around in the truck with my uncle Rick, there were five or six of us, and we drove past the funeral home and he said, "Your uncle Bob's in there."

"He is not, he's in the hospital," I said.

"Your uncle is so, he's dead."

The next day or not long after that, we went to the funeral home and that's when I saw my uncle Bob, and I still couldn't understand that he was dead. My aunt Rainey talked to me at that point, she still had the bandage around her chest — her chest bone had been broken. She couldn't move very well. I saw a lot of pain in her eyes but I couldn't really understand why. When I saw my uncle Bob, who was like a dad to me, I touched him, but it never sunk in that he was dead, not really.

Not long after that, my world changed. It was like seeing a table full of stuff and somebody pulls the tablecloth out from under it and everything still stays on the table. After my uncle's death, my aunt Rainey sank into herself. I moved back with her and we stayed on our own for maybe two months. She got a boyfriend not long after and it felt like it pushed me away. She didn't have time for me anymore. She was never at home. A lot of times I'd come home to an empty house and she wouldn't be home till late. She was with him, having fun going fishing, doing things. I wondered why they didn't include me.

We moved out to a place down River Range. It was again a new stage in my life, but there was no uncle Bob in it. It was a huge two-storey house. A lot of it was blocked off because it was so big and they couldn't use it all. My aunt Rainey felt I was intruding on her relationship because her friend Hank didn't like me. I knew why he didn't like me, because he tried to abuse me. I remember being trained to like it and it shocked him and repulsed him. And of course then I was this little she-devil, but I was just a kid, I just knew I was bad. I think my aunt just wanted me away and he wanted me away but they wanted me there because they knew that they could get money for taking care of me. I don't really know how my aunt felt at that point; she didn't talk to me. I started living in the attic. That's where I stayed and when they didn't want me to come down they would lock the door from the bottom of the stairs. So again, I was living through the TV, they made sure I had a TV up there. I was very isolated at that point. I think I started forming my idea of what I wanted, what was perfect, I knew this wasn't. They would go off fishing and leave me alone, not say a *word*, not say, "Okay, Carol, we're going out." No, they didn't care and then it was Christmastime. I lived that way mid-summer to Christmastime.

That Christmas my aunt Rainey packed me up. I wondered what the heck she was doing. She packed all my good clothes and said, "Oh, we're going to go visit your grandpa." He lived with my uncle Joey and his wife in the homestead up on Town-line. I loved my uncle Joey. I loved my grandfather, he was everything to me, he even let me sleep in his bed. I think I was there maybe three days and I was wondering, "How come my aunt Rainey just brought me and dropped me off? Oh, she'll come for me later." Then I was taken away. I remember that time vividly. I was watching *Heidi* and I had got really emotional when an aunt from Detroit walked in and said, "Are you ready?" It was like something possessed me that wouldn't let me talk, it felt like I was in this other world. I didn't know what she was talking about. I didn't understand what was going on.

She packed me up into this little car and took me to Kitchener. I can remember walking in and I had my prettiest dress on. My leotards had a little hole in them. I walked in the door and there was another aunt, but she said she was my mom, my real birth mother. There was a man with her. He was Native. "Okay," I thought, "I can handle this, whatever is going on." Then I found out I had a brother and sister. This was a whole new world to me. I can remember walking in and standing there, with my box beside me and my mother — I'll call her Mother — looking at me and saying, "I know you're dirty little pigs down there, all you guys you're dressed like that. You never have nothing nice." She was putting down the reserve, putting down ME. Putting down the reserve is putting down me. That's how we live, that's how we act. She made me carry my box out to the incinerator and burn everything in it, bit by bit. Of course what she really did was to symbolize that it was the end. I knew that was it.

I didn't know what to think. Everything flowed along quite quickly. She sat me down with my new stepfather and said, "This is your dad, and this is Mom. You call me Mom. Your aunt and uncle from Detroit want to be your godparents." I was just shaking my head, going along, just trying to survive.

There were three bedrooms in the apartment and me and my sister, who was three years older than me — I didn't know her, I didn't know her at all — we slept together. It wasn't long after that I started realizing something was funny but familiar. My stepfather started coming into the bedroom and he would touch me and I'd sort of drift off to sleep. I'm not sure where it went with that, but it happened on a regular basis. I think it must have been happening before I got there because my sister and I would fight about the edge, because whoever was sleeping on the edge of the bed usually got it. So we would always fight about the edge — we'd fight *not* to lay by the edge. I thought, "Here we go again. Same old thing."

My sister and I really never got along. She must have been thirteen or fourteen, starting to go out and be her own self. I knew she wanted to get away, too, and I didn't know whether that was because of the abuse or not. My brother was three years younger than me. When my sister left one day, I was so mad that she didn't take us. I thought, "You knew it was bad, why didn't you take us?" Then everything was left on my shoulders.

My stepfather was a very demanding man, he was very lazy, *very* physically abusive, plus sexually abusive. I didn't understand, because I wasn't physically abused before that. I couldn't say anything, I couldn't do anything. And I had all these rules. I had to be in bed by 8:00 when I was in high school. I had to have the suppers made. I had to be home at 4:00, precisely at 4:00. If I wasn't at home by 4:00, I knew I had a fist coming. So I learned, I learned. And it made me angry at my sister for leaving me, leaving me all this.

The only happy times I had was when we would go away on trips as "the pretty picture of a family" and I played their game. I got everything I could out of that 'cause that's the only happiness that I really got. When we were home it was a lot different and we weren't sure when we'd get hit, weren't sure what we did to deserve it; it just happened.

I became rebellious, very rebellious. I think I was thirteen in Grade Nine when I met this friend who wasn't a very "good" role model for me. Her family was always drinking. By the time I was in Grade Nine, I wasn't doing too good in school. I knew I wanted school, I knew where I needed to go with it because a long time ago my aunt Rainey had told me, "You live away from this reserve, don't live the life that I'm living. You go away from this reserve and get your education. You come back and you work for your people." She told me this while we were going to get a wine bottle for my uncle Bob. I was so very dependent on that world and I knew I needed my education. But I couldn't cope with what was going on. I needed to get out. I needed to get away. My mother didn't help. She wasn't there for me. I tried to tell her at one point that my stepfather was abusive. What I actually said was, "I don't love my stepfather. I can't love him," and she slapped me across the face. She sided with him. She didn't want to hear anything that I had to say. I became very, very angry.

I got into alcohol first. There were days when I'd rob my piggy bank and go to the liquor store and then go to school drunk. Me and my friend knew how to fix ourselves up to look older. We went through a mickey a day for a while there, and school was starting to slip. I struggled through school. I had hopes and dreams at that point. I knew my education was my "way out," but I still couldn't cope with what was going on at home. My school counsellor sent me to a lady at Waterloo University to talk about my problems. But the whole hour I sat there and cried, there was just so much, I didn't know where to begin. I think it would have worked with her, but my mother found out and I didn't want her knowing about anything that was mine.

I started smoking not long after that. I tried to be a good girl all the time 'cause I knew what I'd get if I wasn't. One day, me and my friends stayed behind the store after it closed and we were smoking. I didn't realize how long we had been there when this police cruiser pulled up and asked which one was Carol, and I jumped into the cruiser. What scared me, what made my heart jump was that I had seen our car pull up behind the cruiser and my stepfather was in it. I told the police officer, "I don't want to go with him. He's going to beat me." And he says, "Well, you can call back." It was like, "Yeah right, you don't want to help me now, fine. I've been through it before, I'll go through it again." I got into my stepfather's car and of course the police officer goes, "Well, Mister, your daughter's saying that she doesn't want to go with you because she's going to get a beating." And, of course, my stepfather's nice as pie, and he says, "Oh no, officer. Everything's just fine. Her mother's going to handle it." Well, my mother handled it all right. I got home and she found an extension cord and beat me with it. That wasn't the worst. I was used to handling pain, but the cord hit me up and down my legs and you could see the cuts where it was bleeding. The worst part and the humiliating part was that they made me go to school, and my stepfather says, "You wear a dress, so everybody can see that you're a bad girl." So of course, I believed that. I didn't believe it was abusive, I just knew I was a bad girl. A teacher asked me about it, but of course, I hid it and told her everything was fine at home. I probably made up an excuse. And I had seen another side to my mother as well — my stepfather had to come in to get her to stop, 'cause she couldn't stop.

That experience with my mother and another beating from my stepfather made me want to leave. I talked to my friend about it. I was trying to find somebody to love me and her brother was there. He was a drunk, but he was there. He showed me a bit of attention and, of course, I didn't think that I was anything, you know, I just knew what I was good for. When me and my friend got drunk she said, "My sister lives in Toronto. Let's go to Toronto." That day, that afternoon, we left. I left a note on the table, saying "Bye." Me and my friend hitchhiked to Toronto to her sister's place. I met up with her brother, who came a couple of days later. Whatever there was to smoke, I smoked, and whatever there was to pop, I popped, and whatever there was to drink, I drank it. I don't remember too much, except allowing myself to be humiliated a lot, by men. I phoned my brother and I told him that I loved him and I missed him and it seemed like he had been mad at me, too, for leaving. We stayed there for almost two months and then me and my boyfriend moved back to Kitchener.

My boyfriend wouldn't talk to me unless he was drinking,

so I made sure that he was always drinking. He physically abused me. One night we got into a fight. He had thought that I was looking at somebody, since I was talking to somebody else, and he grabbed my hand and started punching me. I thought I could always defend myself, why couldn't I? He made me fit into a role that was almost normal, a role I had grown up with and that worked to help me get through my childhood. It felt good, actually.

Another time, I remember running down the road, in the middle of winter. He thought I was cheating on him and had chased me out of the house. It was during an ice storm and we were living only a block away from where my parents lived. He got hold of me and beat the heck right out of me. I ran to some bushes. I didn't have no coat on, no shoes on and I waited till he was gone. I waited for quite awhile; it was pretty cold. I ended up sleeping in the car outside. I snuck in, in the morning, and got my shoes and coat, but then I knew it was time to leave him and I went back to my parents' house.

It was the only place I had and I stayed there for a night and then my stepfather, of course, said to me, "Well, so you smoke and drink now, eh? Well you better stay up with me." He showed me what he wanted to do with me, that's for sure, now that I was a big girl. I left again, the next day. I ended up working in a factory and I found this place where I could rent a room for $97.00 a week. I arranged that through a friend from high school. It was his place. So I lived there for almost three months on my own while I was working. I don't remember too many paycheques, 'cause soon as I got one, it was gone. I saw a lot of people older than me — I could see their lifestyle, where it got them and it sort of worried me. But yet, I felt comfortable, the pain was numbed, everything was gone, there was nothing left. I wasn't in need anymore. I was a nothing.

At that point, my aunt Rainey phoned me from the reserve to say her husband Hank had died, and with the insurance money she was going to Nashville. That was the first time I had talked to her since I left. She asked me if I wanted to go to Nashville with her and I said, "No, I won't leave. I have to go to work." But then things fell apart. I was drinking too much and I ended back up in my parents' house. I stayed one night, and then I wound up my blanket and everything that was personal of mine that I could carry and put it in a bag and left. I hitch-hiked down to the reserve.

I can remember looking in the mirror and wanting to pull my skin off. I wanted to be "white," I wanted to fit in. I wanted to have a relationship, but for some reason I looked different, I couldn't understand how. It had to do with my skin; it had to do with me inside.

When I moved back to the reserve, I stayed with my aunt Rainey, who had come back from Nashville. Me and her got along really good again, and we stayed in the big house together. I was fifteen going on sixteen. I had lived a whole life before I even got there, and that's where I met my husband, whom I'm still married to today. My cousins had already gotten partners. But the training that they had given me didn't go away. When I saw them, they would wait until I got drunk and remind me, and I would slip into the old mind-set that kept me there. And I so much wanted to fight that, but I didn't know how. I thought they had so much power over me.

My partner had just turned fifteen when I met him. Actually, all the time I had been going to that abusive home, he had lived right across the road. He had been right there, but we had never met as children. After we did meet, we started to work on a relationship. He loved me so much, it was smothering to a point, because I felt I didn't deserve that. I needed to detach myself all the time and that's where infidelity came along. In a way it was self-abusive, because I needed to abuse myself to feel normal. Me and my partner moved to the city. I thought we could look for jobs there, but then I got pregnant. I told my partner, "You're too young. I've lived my whole life. I'm a stronger person. I can handle living on my own and having my baby." I went back to my biological mother's house in Kitchener to get on with my life. You know, to get money and try to be independent. He was up there no more than two days later, and he asked me to marry him and I said yes, after the baby's born.

So after our son was born, when he was two months old, we got married on the reserve, but we lived in the city. After having my son, I went through a really hard time with depression. My husband would come home and I would be sitting on the floor pulling my hair out, the baby crying. He didn't understand what was going on. Well, neither did I. We moved, and it got worse and I became suicidal. It got to the point where we started drinking so much that we lost our son. One of my aunts took him because we had no heat and hydro in the middle of winter, but we were drunk. Even the fish froze up in mid-stream. I can remember that. I was too busy getting drunk — I wanted my husband to hurt me so much, but he wouldn't, then I would push him and push him and push him. I wanted him to abuse me like I'd always been and he wouldn't. And then going through the depression and still drinking, I became very suicidal.

We came down to the reserve a lot — 'cause they couldn't take the bush out of us, just couldn't. My aunt Rainey ended up with my husband's dad and they were living together, and they had taken our son in. So when we'd come down to visit, we'd visit all of them and we'd stay there. I think that was the sanction that we needed, in a way. They just loved our son, they just doted on him. I knew my son was safe there. One night we had come down for a house party. I was very depressed and I think I had come to the end. I looked at my son and thought, "All he has to look forward to is being abused. That's all there is in life." And I thought, "Well, I'm not capable of looking after him."

The night that I tried to end it, I knew I had to stay sober, so I only drank a little bit, and I acted drunk. My grandfather and a bunch of people were in the house. I walked right past them and went into the kitchen, opened the drawer, grabbed a knife and stuck it in my pants. I wanted to make it perfect, because I didn't want them to think I was crazy and I didn't want anybody to ruin anything for me. I said, "I'm so tired, I just gotta go lie down." Then I sliced my wrists, stuck the knife in a hole in the wall and went to sleep, hoping never to wake up again. My husband walked in and pulled off the blankets. He thought that I was in bed with my cousin. He said, "What in the hell are you doing here?" He grabbed me and pulled my wrists. I just screamed. He pulled me on the floor and started slapping me, saying, "This is it. You're nothing but a whore!" Then he saw the blood everywhere and said, "What the hell did you do?"

They called the ambulance. I put up a fight, I wasn't going to let nobody take me. They had to tie me down; they had my hands tied behind me; I fought. "Why are you doing this? Why can't you just leave me alone, let me die?" I yelled at them. I got to the hospital and the doctor was angry at me. He stitched me up and didn't give me any anaesthetic. He stitched my wrists up and said, "It's this stupid drunken Indian again." I was trying to disassociate from the pain and I got in the wheelchair and to the waiting room, and there was my husband and all my abusers and their partners. They were all sitting there, so worried about me. I looked at them and I surprised myself. I said,

"What the hell are you guys looking at, the clown at the circus?" I looked at their faces and they couldn't understand why I had become so angry, why I wanted to hurt myself.

I stayed in a mental institution for three weeks. I was in such a haze from the medication that I never really dealt with anything. My husband said to me, "Well, if you do that again, I'm going to leave you." I thought, "Oh, my God, he's going to leave me. The only person who's ever loved me is going to leave me." Then I thought, "Well, if it ends, if the job had been completed, it wouldn't have mattered anyway." We moved back home and it all began again. My son was still with my aunt Rainey. I took two more overdoses within a month. My wrists were still bandaged and the doctor looked at me and said, "If you ever do this again, you know that you can be charged." That scared me, because I had always been taught to listen to people, to listen to authority, and I wondered how can somebody charge you? But I think it shook me enough to see what I was doing to myself.

The social worker came and gave me the first little inkling that I needed. She saw a picture that my uncle Bob had left for me before he passed away. My aunt Rainey had given it to me and it was a picture of the Last Supper. It would change to Jesus kneeling down, if you looked at it in a certain way, when it had a light over it. I was sitting there and the social worker came in and my wrists were bandaged up and she knew that I was in a really bad emotional state. She didn't talk to me like a social worker, she talked to me like a person. She asked me what I had in my life and about my spirituality. I told her about my spirituality and she asked me where I got that from and I told her. Then she said, "Do you think that your uncle Bob would have wanted you to do that? Do you think that your uncle would have wanted you to be living like this?" And she went a really long mile for me. I wanted to be alone, I wanted to just have my son and just be alone, just have peace somewhere. So she worked really hard and she found me a townhouse. But when she came and told me she had found me a place, my husband and I had already decided to move as a couple back to the reserve.

But I was unsure. Should I move there, should I not move there? My truck was all packed and I ended up moving back to the reserve. Of course we kept on drinking, became very abusive to each other. I physically hurt my husband. I regret a lot of that and I still have to live with that. He could have charged me, but he decided not to. It became a not very nice family. There was a lot of drinking, a lot of abuse, a lot of violence. But I still wanted to go out and fulfill those other dreams of mine.

And then I had my daughter and I think she changed my life. My son was three. I had so much wanted a girl. It was like a cycle had come around. This was me again, in some sort of symbolic way. I was going to make a difference for her that my mother didn't make for me. I was going to be there for her. I was going to change things and I did. I just shut everything off. I quit drinking, I didn't allow anybody in my house who drank, I stopped seeing my mother, I stopped phoning her. I became more attached to my aunt Rainey. Not long after, I decided to go back to school. I went to computer training, worked for a K-Mart for two and a half years, worked at a part-time job growing asparagus. I always loved to work the ground, so I worked on a lot of farms through the years to keep food on the table. I had another daughter nine years later.

Then I saw an ad in the paper for a volunteer at a shelter. It outlined all my qualifications and I thought, "I'm gonna do that. I've been through hell-and-back. I want to volunteer." Not thinking that I could do any more than that, I went for my interview and they accepted me as a trainee. I took the full training when the shelter first opened. It was three very intensive weeks. That was the first time in my life that I had seen others who were pained; it wasn't just me. It was shocking. It was coming home and I knew I had a place. Not long after, the woman who did the volunteer training asked me if I wanted to do Life Skills training, and I took that. The combination of looking at my abuse and my learning about humanistic development and how feelings work and learning to put labels and words to things I feel opened my whole world. I couldn't believe it. It was a short period of time but so many intense things happened to me, it was like I was ready for it. I absorbed and I pulled in as much as I could: "Tell me a little bit more, tell me more, I need to find out more." It put a meaning into everything that I had gone through. A friend told me, "Well, maybe you can repay that," and I think that sort of helped me. It became my thing, to be first the victim and now the helper. So I have found my work.

At the time I didn't know how to handle the flashbacks, or how to deal with being around my husband and his family. Two of his sisters married two of my abusers and seeing them at family gatherings and living right near them made me feel very paranoid. I wanted to keep my family safe, keep the abusers away. But I knew I was going to have to meet up with people from my family and how could I deal with that?

I asked if I could come and work at the shelter. They hired me on as part-time and I've been there working part-time relief ever since. I feel very comfortable in my job. Again, working at the shelter was coming back to my identity. Working in this environment and managing the healing aspect is intense. Sometimes you work with groups where you hear a lot of stuff. I run a group for non-offending parents. This is another aspect of my life that I deal with — the pain that I had as a parent, how to deal with the child, how to deal with her pain, how to look at her from a mother's point of view. The guilt that you have there carries on forever. That group is going really, really well. When I walk out after a session, I feel like I'm walking on air. When I started the group, people said, "Oh, you won't get it going, not in this community. It's too, too close, and people won't trust you." But I got it going and it's been working.

When I lead the groups I back off and give them lot of affirmations that they're on the right track. Or I tell them that being a mother is okay. Right from the beginning, I try to let them know that there's no social status in this room, there's no gender bias, there's no racial bias, because we have non-Native and Native parents in the room. We have to look at all that. I always tell them, "I'm here to protect you, as a group. So if there's anything going on, please let me know, we can address that." I try to keep everything very controlled, so that things don't go astray and it's been working well. I always tell them, "Phone me for support if you need it," because a lot of them are dealing with the courts and that can be horrendous. One woman phoned me up and she had never called me, so I was really surprised. She said, "That advice you gave me is hard, but I think it's working." It made me feel that I was on the right track with this group and with the other groups that I work with. I try to back off, but give a little bit of myself in there, make things available, try to bring speakers in, try to have enough information for them, give them support. I go to court with some of them. Being there, just being there, that's how it keeps going.

Working in this environment, in the shelter for abused women on the reserve, I worry about my identity. Am I Indian enough to be here? Am I dark enough? I don't know how to speak the language, does that make me not Indian enough? I don't go to the Longhouse or I haven't been to the Longhouse, does that make me Indian?

I am still prone to depressions, but I've really worked on them. I'm usually down on myself, but then I think, well that's my way of staying humble. Being here — working in the shelter — has put some purpose in my life. What I have to offer from my life experiences, I'm more than willing to give, to help somebody, if she needs the information. I'll do anything I can for her. A lot of my value comes from being a part of a group, which I could never do before, having been so isolated. I feel that I have a lot to give and I have a lot more that I can give. Being a leader is not what you can take, it's what you can give. And if you feel a burden while you're doing a good job as a leader (and sometimes I feel burdened with all the things that I get myself into), you have to keep yourself humble.

I try to develop my spirituality. I didn't know I had a spirit. I think that's my goal right now, to develop the gifts that the Creator has given me and that's the ability to see things in people, to feel their pain and be able to pull that out and talk to them about it. There are Elders who have helped me through this. I try to seek as much information from them as I can and use it, yet still have the workbook knowledge as well. I try to maintain both. So that's where I'm coming from right now, just trying to work my gift and see where it's going.

But I'm looking after myself, too, and being there for my family. My husband's done a lot. The roles are a complete switch — he's standing at the stove and Lana's tugging at him. I'm well looked after.

There's so much to learn. I don't know where I'm going with this but I feel happy where I'm going.

Mirror Dearest, Who Is More Beautiful: The True Me ... Or the Other One?

MONA AZIZ

So she decided to talk to me, and I decided to listen. That was how the dialogue started with my inner self, that true reflection of which I am; that presentation which is at times so present and strong and at other times so distant and obscure.

She needs no introduction or definition, but she wants to talk about her reality — she wants to speak to her experience. Her name isn't important to know although it is as beautiful a name as she is a person. So I decided that I would call her "Foreign Beauty." She comes from a faraway land, described by the people who create boundaries as the "Middle East." She matures every day as a person who was born there but lives here, in Canada. In fact, she remembers no other home and wishes sometimes that there were none.

She says what never occurs to her to say, even in her dreams.

But who will listen, she asks, and who will understand? There is so much sadness in her heart, so much hurt that she wants nothing but to hurt back, even through words. She can't recall a smile from her childhood. She once wrote, in those childhood days, that she was living in a grave. Even in the grave, there were rules to live by, which seemed so unfair. She thought that since it was a grave, there ought to be no rules. It was just like a prison; there were more rules there than on the outside.

Her mother was a gentle, timid Dove who was taken from a home to live in a golden cage. Mind you, one has to qualify the "reality" of that home. See, in that home, she was circumcised, and it is difficult not to allow a human being the right to describe this experience as brutal. But Dove's feelings are her own, and no one should claim them. Yet Dove knew not how to talk about feelings, she could only state facts. She learned not to respond to questions but only to act on them.

As a child, Beauty couldn't understand why Dove was always so sad, why she always wished Beauty was a boy, and why she was grateful that Beauty was an only child. All Beauty knew was that Dove's sadness was passed down to her in every drop of milk her infant body sucked and in every breath she breathed. Every wrinkle on Dove's face, every crumpled tissue in her body, every silenced part of her soul spoke of her experience at "home." Beauty felt that that time of Dove's life was ugly; it was ugly to remember and to re-live, yet so ugly it was impossible to forget.

In that "home," another thorn was planted on Dove's crown — sexual abuse. Beauty didn't know why it happened; it seemed to translate into something about the nature of all men — or men, in general. It certainly painted "family" life with one huge dirty brush, and seated men on the throne of those who bestow pain, and women on that of those who humbly receive it. The father, who sexually abused Dove, also abused her two sisters.

The grandfather that Beauty never saw and never had was her pain from her mother's side.

Few would understand that because Dove lost her freedom so early in life, it didn't matter anymore whether she was caged or not, whether she was dead or alive, whether she could fly or not. Beauty has, in fact, come to understand what happened to her mother. What she could never understand, however, was her father's reactions to Dove's life and his responses to it. Dove had no hope, no expectations and no dreams, but Beauty did. It stood to reason to expect him to be soothing, to wipe the locked-up tears, to tend to the sore heart and to pick up where everybody left off. Needless to say, she wondered why her father didn't do all that.

Beauty thought that maybe she was asking the wrong questions. She started looking for signs of all that he was trying to do to forbid the "great" pain from seeping into his life and into his family's life. But as far as she could remember, Dove lay dead in her cage, while he lay dead outside it. He was dead to all of Dove's needs for understanding, compassion and companionship. But he took good care of his own needs. He looked good and went to functions that allowed him to feel good. He provided the bare necessities of life to his family, which made him a responsible head of a household who did his family a lot of good. It seemed to him that all should be okay, that the world ought to be so grateful to him for all that he had done. Yet Beauty was not grateful. He did not see that the only off-spring that would carry his name had no pride in his acts, thoughts or intentions. Beauty was aware that she was a precious seed that needed nurturing to grow and thrive, but she wasn't sure how much of that she got.

Beauty knew from her life as a growing woman that the caged Dove was almost like a tune that her father simply disliked. It was so easy for him to shut her off, instead of changing the tune. But she wanted to know if they ever had togetherness. Beauty thought that a union between two human beings transforms their lives into a beach that both walk along. Sometimes they jump into the waters and swim and other times they just walk, rest or stand still, and sometimes they have to part to discover different areas of the beach. So she dives into her memory, and searches some more. She remembers sitting on their balcony, like a baby in a mother's belly, trying not to hear the fight between her parents. She tried to forget what her father said that day, but she can't. If it weren't for Beauty, he said, there would have been no family. He wouldn't have lived with the timid Dove.

He wanted an educated lady who could be maid, hostess, good mother, income generator and wife. Now, Beauty smiles and questions herself, has she tried to be all these and more? Only her children, someday, will be able to tell.

Beauty remembers once running away with Dove, using the "hidden" servant staircase. Then after a few hours, coming back to her parents' apartment, to face a father who was angry. The timid Dove said later that he had a knife in his hands, was she right? Beauty will never know. The Dove is so old now that it is no use reminding her of old pains, and Beauty's father is dead. Anyway, it wouldn't matter whether he had a knife or not, both mother and daughter were simply scared. Mother never tried to run away again, and daughter has run away for the longest time from herself, from her memories, from the shameful family history, from a past that she is so afraid to witness again. Beauty dreamed inside her little soul about a different breed from the Dove. As to the damaged image of Man that her spirit has inherited, she has decided to bury it in order to fertilize the ground so she can yield a different breed.

In many ways, Beauty felt she was the only hope for her "family." In fact, she was the only reason for that "family" being together. She took it on herself to take care of it. She was the messenger, the sounding board, the doctor, the diagnosis and the remedy. Now, she can ask herself, at what expense?

Beauty looked for a home to shelter her young self, one that could provide her comfort and safety. The only place she could trust was her own heart. In it, she locked all that she was not supposed to feel, think or envision. She processed everything, in her young heart. She knew that Dove just wanted the cage because she had nothing else to call her own. So even if her castle was one that was built in the air, it was worth keeping. Her father, Beauty knew, wanted to tell the world that he had a golden cage. He wanted a picture of a happy family. In every possible way, she made sure that she never looked happy. Smearing her own image wasn't difficult, since her father was only concerned about providing the bare necessities, and her mother's only way to provide care and at the same time conceal her emotional unavailability was by preparing meals and maintaining the house. Besides, it was a good way to get back at someone. Imagine, the daughter of the nutritionist was fat, the offspring of the perfect family was imperfect.

Beauty breathes deep and continues. As far as her father could see, Beauty had to be worth more than many "boys." She was not to go to the national universities; she had to meet the challenge of foreign education, and so she did. And since they were not that well established, that is financially and economically, she had to work doubly hard for scholarships. She was the statue on the pedestal. She had to overcome and excel in every way to maintain the myth of the happy family. And did she ever!

She learned foreign tongues, visited foreign lands and investigated foreign thought. But Beauty wasn't to love anything she did, let alone anything that was foreign. There was no word in their vocabulary for "fighters" and her house didn't permit them. She used religion to kill the fighter within, and read to the point where even her mentors said it was too much. She sometimes forgot that she existed in a particular space. People existed around her, but she didn't know them. Her family didn't socialize, and she thought it was normal not to relate to others. She went through exams as if they were meals that she had to eat in order to grow. She pulled through her bachelor's degree with a minimum number of people that she called friends. It is important to describe these friends: they were more like the corresponding angles of a triangle. They shared an "equal" mass — equal in quantum and intensity — of pain. They processed it through their souls similarly; that is, they were all melancholic and self-destructive, and they all perceived some form of nobility in all that their lives had to present to them and in how they had to deal with it.

Once the bachelor's degree that her father approved of was completed, she decided to study what she was never allowed to study. That uncivilized self, probably archived because of her "underdeveloped" characteristics, decided that it was time to study what she was all about. It was that self that Beauty felt to be the main focus of her search for any kind of meaning to her life. Beauty knew that she was pregnant with life, but what life was forthcoming from Beauty was beyond her mind's capacity to foresee.

To study philosophy was to tell her world that she was planning to become a "mental" case. To pursue literature was tantamount to declaring herself a "spinster"; and psychology was definitely out of the question — she knew no one who would admit to talking with a psychologist or a psychiatrist. In short, the safest field to be in, as far as Beauty could see, was anthropology. After all, to look at under/developing societies should not be different from looking at an under/developing self. Even then, her father had to come and discuss the "subject" with the department advisors. Was it going to change her? Was she the right material? Would it be of any use to her? Father wanted her to be some approximation of an economist, and a "social" one, who could possibly work in the field of international development. That was the closest he was going to get to what he wanted.

Beauty carried her life with her to work with the "foreigners" in her country. That was how she described the American Experts who claimed to bring development to her land but who ended up taking more than they ever gave. They came young, with very limited experience in their so-called areas of specialization, and with no knowledge on how to respect, protect and contain culture. Beauty was young in years, but as the product of underdevelopment, she was old enough to teach the experts not to undermine the power of the oppressed. She was politically naïve, but working with the experts had an accelerated effect — the politicization of Beauty started; gone was the age of innocence.

On the surface of things, to work with the foreigners was safe in a number of ways. It was prestigious; it was with Christians who might protect their own; it placed her in a tower that sheltered her from the bureaucracy of every day life. Often Beauty felt that she was just the right religion, the right education and the right level of ignorance/idealism that they wanted. Unlike many like her, she marvelled at the possibility of dirtying her hands. Believing that things shouldn't come easily to anyone, she was on a mission to learn about her people the hard way —

by being with them. Her kind of women didn't have to do that. They were to be in offices and pursue real work: the family. Graduates from the American system, which she was, should be arm-chair intellectuals not revolutionaries with an agenda of some sort. But Beauty knew better. She was different. A Persian cat, she could never claim to be. She was more like an alley cat with a lot of class.

Beauty was the medium through which the application of foreign aid was administered; she was the bridge to her people. She got to know her people for the first time. She loved them but hated what poverty did to them. Beauty was the Project Assistant, the Evaluator, the Field Officer and the Social Anthropologist that the people didn't need. But that was what she was to them. They wanted to be protected against hardship — both personal and national — but did not want to take part in the protection plan. They wanted a protector but they did not want that force to change their lives; they wanted a structure onto which they could project their wish for change, yet they were unwilling to change too much. Needless to say, she couldn't be all of that. Instead, she acted as a change agent who resisted reality and envisioned a different one. To some people, Beauty was swimming against the current, and to others, she was a traitor.

Beauty watched her soul seek a creator, and heeded the creator's disbelief at how she was changing. She watched her mind choose the work she did, and witnessed her agony over the desperation of the masses and the hypocrisy of politics. She watched her heart embrace a displaced people, and saw her own experience of displacement. Beauty was a mirror of every reality she lived in, but didn't know what was behind that mirror until she finally met a human who reminded her of what it is to fight.

She didn't believe that the instinctive feeling called love would touch her and that she would respond. She even questioned whether it was love. It was definitely a stubborn force. It was a seizure of every one of her faculties that was receptive to change; one that compounded the impact of her work and studies on her life. It raised within her such a resistance to norms that she once considered sacred and indisputable, and stopped a process of an "arranged" life that she thought was inevitable and terminal. It was a love that translated her life into a language of action, action that never stopped once it started.

Had she known that the changes that overtook her would be more than she could handle, maybe she would have chosen to remain in the grave and stay dormant. Yet, as she looks back over the years, she would do everything she did in exactly the same way given the circumstances at the time. She would fight her fear of a love for a foreign being, a Black man, who are one in the sight of the creator but not in the eyes of Man. She would still stand up to her determination that her time was right, and to her knowledge that she was as much part of creation as was the sunset or the eclipse. Beauty wouldn't change the way she loved, the way she worked or even the way she lived. But she would change the reason for all of that.

Beauty picked up the fight on a foreign land. She went to Africa with the Black man, who latter became her husband. The Mother Continent that somehow and somewhere prepared her roots was again initiating Beauty into this new phase of her life. Looking back on her life, Beauty saw that she had acted as a bridge to her people. However, she also recognized that as her people were formulating what they wanted, so was she. In Africa, she didn't want to be a bridge, because that wasn't what the people there needed. She was conscious that who she really was and what she could really do must be articulated in some other way. In Africa, Beauty decided that her best self-expression would be that of a gently flowing river in which all sorts of life could co-exist. She wanted to learn about life in her new surroundings so she allowed herself to feel every new experience that she could capture, without fear or judgement. She went to places, met people and completely forgot herself. Beauty woke up with the sun, walked her Path throughout the days and ended her nights in the arms of time. For two years, she had to forget her resistance simply because she was met with a stronger one. Those years felt like a complete history, a childhood of discovery, an adolescence of adventure and a maturing into an unknown, complex adulthood.

In Africa, Beauty became ready to be a mother. Motherhood was a state that Beauty never thought she would experience. She floated through its initial beginnings and is still trying to fathom the depth of it all. To carry life was the healthiest thing she had ever done. To bring forth a new being revived every cell in her body, and to pass down life expressed every wave in her soul. In no time, Beauty realized that to actually enjoy her new-born family was a sufficient explanation for a major part of her existence.

In Africa, Beauty tried to complete her Masters in Anthropology through correspondence. She had formulated her theoretical orientation, done her field work and needed to make linkages. She had to show how reality was an application of a socioeconomic concept within a specific model. Yet she had to postpone this until a later time and another phase of her intellectual development. In Africa, she acquired a different model of knowledge; one that was so different to what she was familiar with. And then Beauty had to conclude this phase of learning. Canada offered her, her husband and her daughter a new home.

They were stateless — in political terms — and Canada gave them an opportunity to change that status. For Beauty, Canada granted a status that introduced a lot of change into her life.

How did she live in these foreign lands and adjust, she who had never really learned how to live as a social animal? Maybe, it was the fact that her new life was always different from the one that she was used to. She had to survive, yet it took more than that. It was combat time. She had to spread her wings that were tightly tucked in, and develop a body, mind and soul that befitted the new land.

Throughout her first year of living in Canada, it was not difficult to copy and conform to the image that was printed onto the screen of North American life, especially when it came to the work scene. Beauty thought that she was actually doing so well. Day after day she would see a change in the mirror and would pass it off as a necessary additive to the "cultural concoction" that she would have to get used to. So when she felt uncomfortable with all the references to her being an immigrant, visible minority or a woman of colour, she thought that she was young in her political development and that what she was experiencing was growing pains. When she struggled with her capacity to do Casual Counselling/Vocational Instructing, work on her master's degree, or hold an Assistant Teaching position in addition to her Family Role, she told herself that that would teach her to appreciate the struggles of so-called pioneers and truly understand the "grinder cycle" in the immigrant experience.

Beauty's integrity was at stake. Her sense of wholeness was eroding. The small allowances she made were actually transforming who she was in a very subtle way. She now sees that many of these small acts — for example, making herself accept her work surroundings — were acts of resistance to that work.

Beauty didn't enjoy being five minutes late for work every day but she tried to put that "in context" of how much more time she had to spend preparing for her workday. She couldn't accept being negligent in completing either her work or home duties, but again that was just part of the general experience of working in North America. It was imperfect, but it was okay to be imperfect, since no one puts demands on anybody to be perfect. It was simply enough to learn and to grow. When she finally admitted to stagnation and recognized that she was losing her creative self, that was again a prerequisite to that phenomena called "alienation," which was a normal state of being in a productive workplace.

Those feelings of resentment, helplessness and surrender were part and parcel of a negative attitude towards work and, accordingly, it was urgent to uproot them for the good of everything else. Yes, she didn't appreciate a system that allowed every worker to choose between an ethical and a non-ethical approach to work. In another life, in another world, workers had no choice because work is ethics made visible. It amazed her when she worked in government, that she would work for no pay and that would be called "commitment time": commitment to what, she would ask? And in the non-profit sector, when she did the same, that was called "volunteer time." She certainly couldn't understand how you can work without joy and call that good work. How could a world described as so perfect not help one discover the secret of joy?

So sure was Beauty of her sense of responsibility that there was only one route to continuity — she had to loose it. She had been there before, and subconsciously had no plans to go there again. If she didn't have to forget what she learned while working, she had to forget what she was doing just to continue doing it. She had to remember to leave her work behind her, otherwise, "real" life would pose challenges to some work policies and procedures. It was much safer to keep "living" scenarios out of work in which she strove to address the needs of human beings. As a matter of fact, it was much easier to think of herself as role-playing rather than working. So Beauty was the Efficient Adjudicator, and the Dedicated Community Developer and the Consultant who became aware that everyone in Canada who was educated and looking for work was one.

Beauty learned that although some workplaces appeared to be accommodating, it was expected that family life shouldn't interfere with work. Basically, she had to insulate herself to ensure that she could function under whatever inhuman circumstances she experienced at work. Beauty had to just look around to confirm that she was not different from anybody else, and since everybody else was fighting, to do anything different was wrong. She was obliged to hold on to work for survival, and at the same time look out for other fulfilling jobs. This eternal dichotomy articulated itself as the main feature in Beauty's work life. Many times she wished she could quit working, but it would have cost her family dearly. Her "deep inside," that place that historically hid all her pain, was growing full, however, and she had no clue that that process was making her really sick. And again, it was much easier to follow the old pattern, because that hurt self couldn't be seen by anybody: a perfect disguise.

That strong need within her to hurt, which was as simple in her mind to interpret as distinguishing between good and evil, was still not easy to describe. It was almost like trying to capture a shadow at midday. Trying to trace its origins was hard. But as far back as she could go in memory, whenever she was hurt, either at home or outside it, she couldn't respond to the mounting pain within. She had no right to and definitely wasn't trained to defend herself and stand up for who she was. She could only react by looking at herself for a resolution. Her sweet self would never hurt her back, or be angry at her for acting up, or even tell on her. And when that self sought love and understanding, this simply made Beauty hurt herself even more.

Not only was she hurting herself, but she was spilling her own pain onto the world. She just didn't care anymore because going to work was painful, and so was being part of this world. In her limited capacity, she took over a responsibility that she knew didn't belong to her in the first place. She no longer had to be the single one to pay for all this pain; someone else had to pay — in fact, everyone else should pay. So with this great philosophy as her foundation, Beauty went after everyone she knew and made them pay for every single loss she had ever had to incur.

She couldn't identify all that she did, thought or felt along the way, only some of the things. Beauty honoured some dear aspects of herself, became distant from some and parted with others. She loved her voice — gentle, deep and low. That, she has never given up, even though to some power-hungry figures it was very intimidating, and to some powerless ones it was too weak. But then there were other elements of her personality that she was not comfortable with. One was the sad child who felt that something was inherently wrong with her, and constantly yearned to be better. Another was her juvenile self that got back at the world and who witnessed how angry she was and who captured the anger that she carried over from others. Yet another was that self-less individual whom she so naturally gravitated to be at the expense of being sometimes called the sacrificial lamb or worse. At times, these parts were easy to manipulate. But, alas, there were other times, when she felt that she was dealt a hard hand. To win felt totally valueless in the face of all that she lost.

Beauty tried to tend to her Path. She didn't know that was called "taking care" of oneself in the language of modern individualism. But assimilation interfered so much with her inner process, that Beauty could no longer walk her Path. She missed whole sections of it. She had to continuously revisit some of these, and rework some of the forgotten words and actions. Why did this happen? Beauty is still trying to understand that. Maybe, she was not that well prepared for a life where she called the shots. When the day started, she already had a full agenda and as she went through her day, she continuously had to alter it. When it was time to call it a night, time was powerless and her soul yearned endlessly for more time.

Beauty knows that she has to relearn and regain most of what she lost on the Path before she can finish it. She recalls reaching out and remembers some faces that helped her piece together the lost parts. She also remembers those who declared the pieces weren't worth the effort. Now, she fears what she is. Is she well pieced together or has she undergone so much "alteration" that she is mostly poisonous matter?

Is she comfortable with saying more right now? No, she is not. She is very ashamed; she wants to remain in hiding; no one should be able to recognize Beauty for who she really is. Remember, she is still trying hard to remember who she is. Beauty wants to stop. She wants to stop hurting herself and others. One day, she wants to say more and be heard and not be judged by her own self and by others whom she dearly loves but sometimes hurts.

More than anything, however, she wants to warn other Foreign Beauties that the realities of life in a foreign land can transform them. So much so that they may feel completely estranged from their original selves. As Beauty said at the beginning, she wanted to talk about her life. But she couldn't produce more than the words that are here. She begs me to love what she says, and I do. I do because I know more about Beauty than anybody else.

As I look to Beauty to put some closure on this work, as I see her pain coming out of her open life, I know her words are telling me to accept her and not condemn her. I will keep her wounds hidden and closed until another time when more pain can come out, and until the time when there will be no more pain.

Too Many Choices

TRACY FRANKLIN

Thank you, Dad, for fighting back from the heart attack.
We love you.

Another Journal year has come to its close. This year has shown me many things. Things I need and want to remember. For at times there are too many choices!

1) This has been a year of pro and con lists, at times finding them dead even. Decisions however must be made. I'm choosing the ones where I'm willing to live with the consequences.

2) It's been a year of doing all the "do" things we all have to do. I'm happy to say my average was pretty good for getting them done.

3) It's been a year of cutting losses. They've been extremely heavy this year. Instead of getting "stuck" there, though, I've realized that with loss can come new beginnings. This is what I choose to focus on. Times can be really hard, but worse if I choose to "live" there.

4) Life is change, good and bad. Some changes I've deemed necessary. Others I've found are people's decisions and circumstance dictating to me. This can be frustrating, but there is also the light of new adventure if I reach to turn it on. I choose to

reach! If left unattended, I know it would all grow too big for me in the dark.

This year I've learned I will continue my journey no matter what. I'm learning when to give, when to let go and to accept reality. I've learned I have family and "forever friends" (those wonderful few that I just know and love that I'm stuck with). I've learned to cherish my daughters and to take time to watch carefully their daily struggles into womanhood. Finally, I've learned (after thirty-three years) that I have a mom. She never *really* left, but still I couldn't find her. That is, until I *really* chose to look.

I guess when all is said and done, too many choices are just fine!

Bibliography

Addiction

Addiction Research Foundation. *The Hidden Majority: A Guidebook on Alcohol and Other Drug Issues for Counsellors Who Work with Women.* Toronto: Addiction Research Foundation, 1996.

Adrian, Manuella, et al., eds. *Women's Use of Alcohol, Tobacco and Other Drugs in Canada.* Toronto: Addiction Research Foundation, 1996.

Allen, Chaney. *I'm Black and I'm Sober: The Timeless Story of a Woman's Journey Back to Sanity.* Center City, MN: Hazelden, 1978.

Amethyst Women's Addiction Centre. *Here's to You, Sister: Creating a Women's Addiction Service: Amethyst's Story.* Ottawa: Amethyst Women's Addiction Centre, 1995.

Covington, Stephanie. *A Woman's Way Through the Twelve Steps.* Center City, MN: Hazelden, 1994.

______. *A Woman's Journal: Helping Women Recover. A Program for Treating Substance Abuse. Special Edition for use in the Criminal Justice System.* San Francisco: Jossey-Bass Publishers, 1999.

Kasl, Charlotte Davis. *Many Roads, One Journey: Moving Beyond the 12 Steps.* New York: Harper Perennial, 1992.

Kus, Robert J. *Addiction and Recovery in Gay and Lesbian Persons.* New York: Harrington Park Press, 1995.

Aging

Cobb, Janine O'Leary. *Understanding Menopause.* Toronto: Key Porter Books, 1996.

Doress-Worters, Paula B., and Diana Laskin Siegal. *The New Ourselves, Growing Older: Women Aging with Knowledge and Power.* New York: Touchstone, 1994.

Greer, Germaine. *The Change: Women, Ageing and the Menopause.* Toronto: Knopf, 1992.

Lowes, Catherine D. Rev. ed. *A Seven Step Program for Getting Through Menopause and Enjoying a Longer, Healthier Life, Without Drugs.* Toronto: Health Issues, 1998.

Macdonald, Barbara with Cynthia Rich. *Look Me in the Eye: Old Women, Aging and Ageism.* Duluth, MN: Spinsters Ink, 1983.

Malmo, Cheryl, and Toni Suzuki Laidlaw, eds. *Consciousness Rising: Women's Stories of Connection and Transformation.* Charlotettown: Gynergy Books, 1999.

Mandell, Judy. *What to Expect in Your Fifties: A Woman's Guide to Health, Vitality, and Longevity.* New York: Dell Publishing, 1998.

Marshall, Doris. *Silver Threads: Critical Reflections on Growing Old.* Toronto: Between the Lines, 1987.

Montreal Health Press. *Menopause: A Well-Woman Book.* Toronto: Second Story Press, 1995.

Mudry, Andrea. *World Enough and Time: Conversations with Canadian Women at Midlife.* Toronto: Dundurn Press, 1996.

Neering, Rosemary, and Marilyn McCrimmon. *Facing Changes, Finding Freedom: Canadian Women at Midlife.* Vancouver: Whitecap Books, 1996.

Nickerson, Betty. *Old and Smart: Women and the Adventure of Aging.* Madeira Park, BC: Harbour Publishing, 1995.

Page, Lafern. *Menopause and Emotions: Making Sense of Your Feelings When Your Feelings Make No Sense.* Chicago: Primavera, 1994.

Park, Merri Lu. *Menopause: Time for a Change.* Vancouver: Alive, 1997.

Sang, Barbara, Joyce Warshow, and Adrienne J. Smith. *Lesbians at Midlife: The Creative Transition.* Duluth, MN: Spinsters Ink, 1991.

Anti-Poverty

Baxter, Sheila. *A Child Is Not A Toy: Voices of Children in Poverty.* Vancouver: New Star, 1993.

_____. *No Way to Live: Poor Women Speak Out.* Vancouver: New Star, 1995.

_____. *Still Raising Hell: Poverty, Activism and Other True Stories.* Vancouver: Press Gang, 1997.

Capponi, Pat. *Dispatches from the Poverty Line.* Toronto: Penguin, 1997.

_____. *The War At Home: An Intimate Portrait of Canada's Poor.* Toronto: Viking, 1999.

Cross-Cultural

Agnew, Vijay. *Resisting Discrimination: Women from Asia, Africa, and the Caribbean and the Women's Movement in Canada.* Toronto: University of Toronto Press, 1995.

Ahmed, Leila. *A Border Passage: From Cairo to America — A Woman's Journey.* New York: Farrar, Straus and Giroux, 1999.

Aziz, Nurjehan. *Her Mother's Ashes and Other Stories by South Asian Women in Canada and the US.* Toronto: TSAR, 1994.

Black Girls, The, eds. *Black Girl Talk.* Toronto: Sister Vision Press, 1995.

Bose, Mandakranta. *The World My Mother Gave Me: Asian Women's Perspectives and Perceptions in Literature.* Vancouver: University of British Columbia, Institute of Asian Research, 1998.

Bristow, Peggy, ed. *"We're Rooted Here and They Can't Pull Us Up": Essays in African Canadian Women's History.* Toronto: University of Toronto Press, 1994.

Fife, Connie, ed. *The Colour of Resistance: A Contemporary Collection of Writing by Aboriginal Women.* Toronto: Sister Vision Press, 1993.

Palmer, Hazelle, ed. *"...but where are you really from?" Stories of Identity and Assimilation in Canada.* Toronto: Sister Vision Press, 1997.

Perreault, Jeanne, and Sylvia Vance, eds. *Writing the Circle: Native Women of Western Canada.* Edmonton: NeWest Press, 1997.

Rafiq, Fauzia. *Aurat Durbar: Writings by South Asian Women..* Toronto: Second Story Press, 1995.

Sadler, Rosemary. *Leading the Way: Black Women in Canada.* Toronto: Umbrella, 1994.

Scane, Joyce. *I've Something to Tell You: Stories of Immigrant Women.* Toronto: Seacraft, 1998.

Silman, Janet. *Enough is Enough: Aboriginal Women Speak Out.* Toronto: Women's Press, 1987.

Smith-Ayala, Emilie. *The Granddaughters of Ixmucané: Guatemalan Women Speak.* Toronto: Women's Press, 1991.

Swartz, Sarah Silberstein, and Margie Wolfe, eds. *From Memory to Transformation: Jewish Women's Voices.* Toronto: Second Story Press, 1998.

Disability

Barb Wire Collective. *Not All Violins: Spiritual Resources by Women with Disabilities and Chronic Illnesses.* Toronto: United Church, 1997.

Browne, Susan E., Debra Connors, and Nanci Stern. *With the Power of Each Breath: A Disabled Women's Anthology.* Pittsburgh: Cleis Press, 1985.

Driedger, Diane, and Susan Gray, eds. *Imprinting Our Image: An International Anthology by Women With Disabilities.* Charlottetown: Gynergy Books, 1992.

Driedger, Diane, Irene Feika, and Eileen Girón Batres. *Across Borders: Women with Disabilities Working Together.* Charlottetown: Gynergy Books, 1992.

Kaufman, Miriam. *Easy for You to Say: Q & As for Teens Living with Chronic Illness or Disability.* Toronto: Key Porter Books, 1995.

Klein, Bonnie Sherr. In collaboration with Persimmon Blackbridge. *Slow Dance: A Story of Stroke, Love and Disability.* Toronto: Alfred A. Knopf, 1997.

Mukti, Jain Campion. *The Baby Challenge: A Handbook on Pregnancy for Women with a Physical Disability.* New York: Routledge, 1990.

Nagler, Mark, and Adam Nagler. *What's Stopping You? Living Successfully with a Disability.* Toronto: Stoddart Publishers, 1999.

Ontario Women's Directorate. *Young Girls Talk Disability.* Toronto: Ontario Women's Directorate, 1996.

Solden, Sari. *Women with Attention Deficit Disorder: Embracing Disorganization in the Home and Workplace.* Grass Valley, CA: Underwood Books, 1995.

Willmuth, Mary, and Lillian Holcomb, eds. *Women with Disabilities: Found Voices.* Binghamton, NY: Harrington Park Press, 1993.

Economic Well-Being

Broussard, Cheryl D. *Black Woman's Guide to Financial Independence: Smart Ways to Take Charge of Your Money, Build Wealth, and Achieve Financial Security.* New York: Viking Penguin, 1996.

Cimoroni, Sandy, et al. *Retirement Strategies for Women: Turning Your Dreams into Realities.* Toronto: Key Porter Books, 1997.

_____. *Women in the Know: How to Build a Strategy to Achieve Financial Success.* Toronto: Key Porter Books, 1997.

Ealy, Dr. C. Diane, and Dr. Kay Lesh. *Our Money, Ourselves: Redesigning Your Relationship with Money.* New York: American Management Association, 1999.

Godfrey, Joline. With a Foreword by Gloria Steinem. *No More Frogs to Kiss: 99 Ways to Give Economic Power to Girls.* New York: HarperBusiness, 1995.

Leatherdale, Linda. *Money is a Girl's Best Friend: How Women Can Build Up Assets, Trim Debt and Reap the Rewards.* Toronto: Turnerbooks, 1998.

Lieberman, Annette, and Vicki Lindner. *The Money Mirror: How Money Reflects Women's Dreams, Fears, and Desires.* New York: Allworth Press, 1996.

MacFarlane, Lynne, and Betty Jane Wylie. *Everywoman's Money Book.* Toronto: Key Porter Books, 1995.

Ricciutelli, Luciana, June Larkin, and Eimear O'Neill, eds. *Confronting the Cuts: A Sourcebook for Women in Ontario.* Toronto: York University, Inanna Publications and Education, Inc., 1998.

Smid, Madelon, and Barbara Thrasher. *Smart Women: Canadian Entrepreneurs Talk About Making Money, Leadership, Management and Self Development.* Toronto: Macmillan, 1998.

Stienstra, Deborah, and Barbara Roberts. *Strategies for the Year 2000: A Woman's Handbook.* Halifax: Fernwood, 1995.

Townson, Monica. *Independent Means: A Canadian Woman's Guide to Pensions and a Secure Financial Future.* Toronto: Macmillan, 1997.

Yaccato, Joanne Thomas. *Balancing Act: A Canadian Women's Financial Success Guide.* Toronto: Prentice Hall, 1995.

Yaccato, Joanne Thomas, and Paula Jubinville. *Raising Your Business: A Canadian Women's Guide to Entrepreneurship.* Toronto: Prentice Hall, 1998.

Education

Artz, Sibylle. *Sex, Power, and the Violent School Girl.* Toronto: Trifolium, 1997.

Bailey, Karen R. *The Girls Are the Ones with the Pointy Nails: An Exploration of Children's Conceptions of Gender.* London, ON: The Althouse Press, 1993.

Crozier, Sharon, et al., eds. *Women, Girls and Achievement.* North York, ON: Captus, 1993.

Dagg, Anne Innis, et al., eds. *Women's Experience/Women's Education.* Waterloo, ON: Otter, 1991.

Horsman, Jenny. *"Something in My Mind Besides the Everyday": Women and Literacy in Nova Scotia.* Toronto: Women's Press, 1990.

Hughes, K. Wind, and Linda Wolf. *Daughters of the Moon, Sisters of the Sun: Young Women and Mentors on the Transition to Womanhood.* Gabriola Island, BC: New Society, 1997.

Lloyd, Betty-Ann. *Discovering the Strength of Our Voices: Women and Literacy Programs.* Toronto: Canadian Congress for Learning Opportunities for Women, 1991.

Lloyd, Betty-Ann, Frances Ennis, and Tannis Atkinson. *The Power of Woman-Positive Literacy Work: Program-Based Action Research.* Toronto: Canadian Congress for Learning Opportunities for Women, 1994.

_____. *Women in Literacy Speak: The Power of Woman-Positive Literacy Work.* Toronto: Canadian Congress for Learning Opportunities for Women, 1994.

Macbeth, Fiona, and Nic Fine. *Playing with Fire: Creative Conflict Resolution for Young Adults.* Gabriola Island, BC: New Society Publishers, 1995.

Murch, Muriel. *Journey in the Middle of the Road: One Woman's Path Through A Midlife Education.* Portland, OR: Sibyl Publications, 1995.

Ontario Women's Directorate and the African Heritage Educators' Network. *Succeeding Young Sisters: A Guide to the Development of After-School Encouragement and Mentoring Programs for Young Black Women.* Toronto: Ontario Women's Directorate, 1996.

Food Issues/Body Image

Apostolides, Marianne. *Inner Hunger: A Young Woman's Struggle through Anorexia and Bulimia.* New York: Norton, 1998.

Brown, Catrina, and Karin Jasper, eds. *Consuming Passions: Feminist Approaches to Weight Preoccupation and Eating Disorders.* Toronto: Second Story Press, 1993.

Claude-Pierre, Peggy. *The Secret Language of Eating Disorders: How You Can Work to Cure Anorexia and Bulimia.* Toronto: Vintage Canada, 1997.

Friedman, Sandra. *When Girls Feel Fat: Helping Girls Through Adolescence.* Toronto: HarperCollins, 1997.

_____. *Just For Girls: Facilitator's Manual. A Program to Help Girls Safely Navigate the Rocky Road through Adolescence and Avoid Pitfalls Such As Eating Disorders and Preoccupation with Food and Weight.* Vancouver: Salal Books, 1999.

Hall, Lindsay, and Monika Ostroff. *Anorexia Nervosa: A Guide to Recovery.* Carlsbad, CA: Gürze Books, 1999.

Hirschmann, Jane R., and Carol H. Munter. *Overcoming Overeating.* New York: Fawcett Columbine, 1988.

_____. *When Women Stop Hating Their Bodies: Freeing Yourself from Food and Weight Obsessions.* New York: Fawcett Columbine, 1995.

Hutchinson, Marcia Germaine. *Transforming Body Image: Learning to Love the Body You Have.* Freedom, CA: The Crossing Press, 1985.

Johnson, Carol A. *Self-Esteem Comes in all Sizes.* New York: Doubleday, 1996.

Orbach, Susan. *Fat Is A Feminist Issue: The Anti-Diet Guide to Permanent Weight Loss.* New York: Berkely Books, 1994.

Poulton, Terry. *No Fat Chicks: How Women are Brainwashed to Hate Their Bodies and Spend Their Money.* Toronto: Key Porter Books, 1996.

Saillant, Francine. Trans. Myriam Jarsky. *Interior Passages: Obesity and Transformation.* Toronto: Second Story Press, 1996.

Tremblay, Kimberly Ann. *Eating for the Hell-th of It!: The Complete Nutritionally-Balanced Eating Program Designed Especially for Women.* Deep River, ON: KT-Advantage, 1994.

Wolf, Naomi. *The Beauty Myth.* New York: Vintage, 1997.

Healing and Recovery

Alderman, Tracy. *The Scarred Soul: Understanding and Ending Self-Inflicted Violence.* Oakland, CA: New Harbinger Publications, 1998.

Anderson, Kim. *A Recognition of Being: Reconstructing Native Womanhood.* Toronto: Second Story Press, Forthcoming 2000.

Arnott, Joanne. *Breasting the Waves: On Writing and Healing.* Vancouver: Press Gang, 1995.

Bass, Ellen, and Laura Davis. 3rd rev. ed. *The Courage to Heal: A Guide for Women Survivors of Child Sexual Abuse.* New York: HarperCollins, 1994.

______. *Beginning to Heal: A First Book for Survivors of Child Sexual Abuse.* New York: HarperPerennial, 1993.

Braswell, Linda. *Quest for Respect: A Healing Guide for Survivors of Rape.* Ventura, CA: Pathfinder, 1992.

Brook, Paula. *Work Less, Live More: A Woman's Guide.* Toronto: Doubleday, 1997.

Davis, Laura. *The Courage to Heal Workbook: For Women and Men Survivors of Child Sexual Abuse.* New York: HarperPerennial, 1990.

Enns, Greg, and Jan Black. *It's Not Okay Anymore: Your Personal Guide to Ending Abuse, Taking Charge, and Loving Yourself.* Oakland, CA: New Harbinger Publications, 1997.

Gandy, Debrena Jackson. *Sacred Pampering Principles: An African-American Woman's Guide to Self-Care and Inner Renewal.* New York: William Morrow and Company, 1997.

hooks, bell. *Sisters of the Yam: Black Women and Self-Recovery.* Toronto: Between the Lines, 1993.

Maltz, Wendy, and Beverly Holman. *Incest and Sexuality: A Guide to Understanding and Healing.* San Francisco: Lexington Books, 1987.

Maltz, Wendy. *The Sexual Healing Journey: A Guide for Survivors of Sexual Abuse.* New York: HarperPerennial, 1991.

Native Women's Writing Circle, eds. *Into the Moon: Heart, Mind, Body, Soul.* Toronto: Sister Vision Press, 1996.

Nelson, Jane, Riki Intner, and Lynn Lott. *Positive Discipline for Parenting in Recovery: A Guide to Help Recovering Parents.* Rocklin, CA: Prima Publishing, 1996.

NiCarthy, Ginny. 15th Anniversary Edition. *Getting Free: You Can End Abuse and Take Back Your Life.* Seattle, WA: Seal Press, 1997.

Terichow, Gladys. *Mom's OK: Women in Search of Wholeness.* Winnipeg, MB: North End Women's Resource Centre, 1997.

Woodman, Marion, and Elinor Dickson. *Dancing in the Flames.* New York: Vintage, 1997.

Incest/Battering/Rape/Sexual Abuse/Violence

Agney, Vijay. *In Search of a Safe Place: Abused Women and Culturally Sensitive Services.* Toronto: University of Toronto Press, 1998.

Agtuca, Jacqueline R. *A Community Secret: For the Filipina in an Abusive Relationship.* Seattle, WA: Seal Press, 1994.

Alleyne, Vanessa. *Crazy: A Black Woman's Story of Incest.* Toronto: Sister Vision Press, 1996.

Anderson, Vera. *A Woman Like You: The Face of Domestic Violence. Photographs and Interviews.* Seattle, WA: Seal Press, 1997.

Brazilli, Susan, and Kathleen Gallivan. *Sexual Assault: A Guide to the Criminal System.* Toronto: Metro Toronto Action Committee on Violence Against Women and Children, 1994.

Brewster, Susan. *To Be An Anchor In the Storm: A Guide for Families and Friends of Abused Women.* New York: Ballantine, 1997.

Caffaro, John V., and Allison Conn-Caffaro. *Sibling Abuse Trauma: Assessment and Intervention Strategies for Children, Families, and Adults.* Binghamton, NY: The Haworth Maltreatment and Trauma Press, 1998.

Danica, Elly. *Don't: A Woman's Word.* Charlottetown: Gynergy Books, 1988.

_____. *Beyond Don't: Dreaming Past the Dark.* Charlottetown: Gynergy Books, 1997.

DeKeseredy, Walter, and Martin D. Schwartz. *Women Abuse on Campus: Results from the Canadian National Survey.* Thousand Oaks, CA: Sage, 1998.

Duffy, Ann, and Julianne Momirov. *Family Violence: A Canadian Introduction.* Toronto: James Lorimer and Co., 1997.

Ellis, Megan. *Surviving Procedures After a Sexual Assault.* Vancouver: Press Gang, 1988.

Herman, Judith. *Trauma and Recovery: The Aftermath of Violence — From Domestic Abuse to Political Terror.* New York: Basic Books, 1997.

Johnson, Holly. *Dangerous Domains: Violence Against Women in Canada.* Toronto: Nelson Canada, 1996.

Johnson, Janis Tyler. *Mothers of Incest Survivors: Another Side of the Story.* Bloomington: Indiana University Press, 1992.

Kilgore, Nancy. *Sourcebook for Working with Battered Women.* Volcano, CA: Volcano Press, 1992.

Langlois, Tish. *Fault Lines: Incest, Sexuality and Catholic Family Culture.* Toronto: Second Story Press, 1997.

Levy, Barrie. *Dating Violence: Young Women in Danger.* Seattle, WA: Seal Press, 1998.

Martin, Fern. *A Narrow Doorway: Women's Stories of Escape from Abuse.* Burstown, ON: General Store Publishing House, 1996.

McMaster, Susan, ed. *Siolence: Essays on Women, Violence, and Silence.* Kingston, ON: Quarry Press, 1995.

Neal, L. *Voices of Survivors.* Winnipeg, MB: North End Women's Resource Centre, 1995.

Pearson, Patricia. *When She Was Bad: Violent Women and the Myth of Innocence.* Toronto: Random House, 1997.

Pierce-Baker, Charlotte. *Surviving the Silence: Black Women's Stories of Rape.* New York: Norton, 1998.

Ramsey, Martha. *Where I Stopped: Remembering an Adolescent Rape.* New York: A Harvest Book, 1995.

Renzetti, Claire M., and Charles Harvey Milley, eds. *Violence in Gay and Lesbian Domestic Partnerships.* Binghamton, NY: Harrington Park Press, 1996.

Ross, Samson. *Tough Target: Every Woman's Guide to Personal Safety.* Vancouver: Samson Ross, 1994.

Steed, Judy. *Our Little Secret: Confronting Child Sexual Abuse in Canada.* Toronto: Vintage Canada, 1995.

Timmins, Leslie, ed. *Listening to the Thunder: Advocates Talk About the Battered Women's Movement.* Vancouver: Women's Research Centre, 1995.

Toronto Women's Bookstore. *Books on Violence Against Women and Children: Selected Readings.* Toronto: Toronto Women's Bookstore, 1999.

White, Evelyn C. 2nd ed. *Chain, Chain, Change: For Black Women in Abusive Relationships.* Seattle, WA: Seal Press, 1994.

Wilson, Melba. *Crossing the Boundary: Black Women Survive Incest.* Seattle, WA: Seal Press, 1994.

YWCA of/du Canada. *There's No Excuse for Abuse: Violence Against Women.* Toronto: YWCA of/du Canada, 1993.

_____. *Fresh Start.* Toronto: YWCA of/du Canada, 1995.

_____. *Taking Action on Violence in the Lives of Young Women.* Toronto: YWCA of/du Canada, 1995.

Journals/Writing

Aldrich, Anne H. *Notes From Myself: A Guide to Creative Journal Writing.* New York: Caroll and Graf, 1998.

Coxe, Paula P. *Breathing Space: A Journal for Women Who Do Too Much.* Naperville, IL: Sourcebooks, 1998.

DeSalvo, Louise. *Writing As A Way of Healing: How Telling Our Stories Transforms Our Lives.* San Francisco: HarperSan Francisco, 1999.

Doane, Sharon. *New Beginnings: A Creative Writing Guide for Women Who Have Left Abusive Partners.* Seattle, WA: Seal Press, 1996.

Edmondson, Judy. *Changes: A Woman's Journal of Self-Awareness and Personal Planning.* Santa Barbara, CA: Advocacy Press, 1993.

Lesléa, Newman. *Writing from the Heart: Inspiration and Exercises for Women Who Want to Write.* Freedom, CA: The Crossing Press, 1993.

Schiwy, Marlene. *A Voice of Her Own: Women and the Journal Writing Experience.* New York: Simon and Schuster Trade, 1996.

Shaw, Lucy. *Life Path: Personal and Spiritual Growth Through Journal Writing.* Sisters, OR: Multnomah Publishers, Inc., 1991.

Wylie, Betty Jane. *Reading Between the Lines: The Diaries of Women.* Toronto: Key Porter Books, 1995.

Law

Adelberg, Ellen. *In Conflict With the Law: Women and the Canadian Justice System.* Vancouver: Press Gang, 1993.

Boritch, Helen. *Fallen Women: Female Crime and Criminal Justice in Canada.* Toronto: ITP Nelson, 1997.

Boyd, Susan E. *Challenging the Public/Private Divide: Feminism, Law, and Public Polity.* Toronto: University of Toronto Press, 1997.

Comack, Elizabeth. *Women in Trouble: Connecting Women's Law Violations to Their Histories of Abuse.* Halifax: Fernwood, 1996.

Dawson, T.B., ed. *Relating to Law: A Chronology of Women and Law in Canada.* Noth York, ON: Captus, 1995.

_____. *Women, Law and Social Change: Core Readings and Current Issues.* North York, ON: Captus, 1998.

Faith, Karlene. *Unruly Women: The Politics of Confinement and Resistance.* Vancouver: Press Gang, 1993.

Mothers on Trial. *Family Violence = Family Law Violence: Women's Experience in Family Law Proceedings.* Toronto: Mothers on Trial, 1993.

Rushton, Alfred, ed. *Words from Inside/Les mots de l'Intérieur.* Volume 12. *The Annual Anthology of Prison Arts Foundation.* Brantford, ON: Crown Printing Services, 1992.

Sommers, Evelyn K. *Voices from Within: Women in Conflict With the Law.* Toronto: University of Toronto Press, 1995.

Yogis, John A., Randall R. Duplak, and J. Royden Trainor, eds. *Sexual Orientation and Canadian Law: An Assessment of the Law Affecting Lesbian and Gay Persons.* Toronto: Edmond Montgomery Publications, Ltd., 1996.

Mental Health/Psychology

Bingham, Mindy, and Sandy Stry Ker. *Things Will Be Different for My Daughter: A Practical Guide to Building Her Self-Esteem and Self-Reliance.* Toronto: Penguin, 1995.

Brown, Lyn Mikel, and Carol Gilligan. *Meeting at the Crossroads: Women's Psychology and Girls' Development.* New York: Ballantine Books, 1992.

Blackbridge, Persimmon, and Sheila Gilhooly. *Still Sane.* Vancouver: Press Gang, 1985.

Boyd, Julia A. *In the Company of My Sisters: Black Women and Self-Esteem.* Toronto: Penguin Books, 1993.

Capponi, Pat. *Upstairs in the Crazy House: The Life of a Psychiatric Survivor.* Toronto: Viking, 1992.

Copeland, Mary Ellen. *The Depression Workbook: A Guide for Living with Depression and Manic Depression.* Oakland, CA: New Harbinger Publications, Inc., 1992.

Danquah, Meri Nana-Ama. *Willow Weep for Me: A Black Woman's Journey through Depression.* New York: One World/Ballantine Publishing Group, 1998.

De Rosis, Helen. Rev. ed. *Women and Anxiety: A Step-by-Step Program for Managing Anxiety and Depression.* New York: Heatherleigh Press, 1998.

Funk, Wendy. *"What Difference Does It Make?" The Journey of a Soul Survivor.* Cranbrook, BC: Wild Flower Publishing, 1998.

Hryniuk, Angela. *No Visual Scars.* Victoria: Polestar Books, 1993.

Lerner, Harriet. *The Dance of Intimacy: A Woman's Guide to Courageous Acts of Change in Key Relationships.* New York: HarperPerennial, 1990.

_____. *Life Preservers: Good Advice When You Need It Most.* New York: HarperPerennial, 1996.

Mitchell, Angela, with Kennise Herring. *What the Blues Is All About: Black Women Overcoming Stress and Depression.* New York: Perigee Books, 1998.

Orenstein, Peggy. *SchoolGirls: Young Women, Self-Esteem and the Confidence Gap.* New York: Anchor Books, 1994.

Sanford, Linda T., and Mary Ellen Donovan. *Women and Self-Esteem: Understanding and Improving the Way We Think and Feel About Ourselves.* Toronto: Penguin, 1984.

Shimrat, Irit. *Call Me Crazy: Stories from the Mad Movement.* Vancouver: Press Gang, 1997.

Steinem, Gloria. *Revolution from Within: A Book of Self-Esteem.* Toronto: Little, Brown, 1992.

Mothering

Arnup, Katherine, ed. *Lesbian Parenting: Living with Pride and Prejudice.* Charlottetown: Gynergy Books, 1995.

Beal, Anne C., Linda Villarosa, and Allison Abner. *The Black Parenting Book: Caring for Our Children in the First Five Years.* New York: Broadway Books, 1999.

Bell-Scott, Patricia, Beverly Guy-Sheftall, Jacqueline Jones Royster, Janet Sims-Wood, Miriam DeCosta-Willis, and Lucille P. Fultz, eds. *Double Stitch: Black Women Write About Mothers and Daughters.* New York: HarperPerennial, 1991.

Cohen-Sander, Roni, and Michelle Silver. *"I'm Not Mad, I Just Hate You!" A New Understanding of Mother-Daughter Conflict: Surviving and Thriving During Your Daughter's Teenage Years.* Toronto: Viking, 1999.

Delisle, Deb, and Jim Delisle. *Growing Good Kids: 28 Activities to Enhance Self-Awareness, Compassion, and Leadership.* Minneapolis: Free Spirit Publishing, 1996.

Hanton, Ruth. *Times Two: A Prenatal Guide for the Active Woman.* Ottawa: Serious Fun, 1996.

Herst, Charney, with Lynette Padwa. *For Mothers of Difficult Daughters.* Toronto: Random House, 1998.

Jackson, Marni. *The Mother Zone: Love, Sex and Laundry in the Modern Family.* Toronto: MacFarlane, Walter and Ross, 1992.

Jensen, Larry, and Janet Jensen. *Family Feminism.* Calgary: Detselig, 1994.

Kitzinger, Sheila. *The Year After Childbirth: Surviving and Enjoying the First Year of Motherhood.* Toronto: HarperCollins, 1994.

Lakusiak, Ellen. *Eating Well When You're Pregnant: A Guide to Nutrition for Expecting and Nursing Mothers.* Toronto: Macmillan, 1996.

Lerner, Harriet. *The Mother Dance: How Children Change Your Life.* New York: HarperPerennial, 1998.

Mattes, Jane. *Single Mothers By Choice: A Guidebook for Single Women Who are Considering or Have Chosen Motherhood.* Toronto: Random House, 1997.

Nelson, Fiona. *Lesbian Motherhood: An Exploration of Canadian Lesbian Families.* Toronto: University of Toronto Press, 1996.

Placksin, Sally. *Mothering the New Mother.* Toronto: Key Porter Books, 1995.

Stevens, Patricia, ed. *Between Mothers and Sons: Women Writers Talk About Having Sons and Raising Men.* New York: Scribner, 1999.

Physical Health

Boston Women's Health Collective. *The New Our Bodies Our Selves For the New Century.* New York: Simon and Schuster, 1998.

Bolaria, B. Singh, and Rosemary Bolaria, eds. *Women, Medicine and Health.* Halifax: Fernwood, 1994.

Breen, Mary. *Taking Care: A Handbook About Women's Health.* Toronto: McGraw, 1991.

Callwood, June. *Trial Without End: A Shocking Story of Women and AIDS.* Toronto: Ballantine, 1996.

Currie, Dawn H., and Valerie Raoul, eds. *The Anatomy of Gender: Women's Struggle for the Body.* Ottawa: Carleton University Press, 1992.

Delgado, Jane L. *¡Salud! A Latinas Guide to Total Health — Body, Mind, and Spirit.* New York: HarperCollins, 1997.

DeMarco, Carolyn. *Take Charge of Your Body: Women's Health Advisor.* Aurora, ON: Well Women, 1996.

Dua, Enakshi, et al., eds. *On Women Healthsharing.* Toronto: Women's Press, 1994.

Dunnavant, Sylvia. *Celebrating Life: African American Women Speak Out About Breast Cancer.* Dallas, TX: USFI Inc., 1995.

Federation of Feminist Women's Health Centers. *A New View of A Woman's Body: A Fully Illustrated Guide.* Los Angeles, CA: Feminist Health Press, 1991.

Galambos, Aniko. *An Unexpected Journey: Women's Voices of Hope After Breast Cancer.* Charlottetown: Gynergy Books, 1998.

Hatcher-Roberts, Janet, and C. Vlassot, eds. *The Female Client and the Health-Care Provider.* Ottawa: IDRC Books, 1995.

Kitts, Jennifer, and Janet Hatcher-Roberts. *The Health Gap: Beyond Pregnancy and Reproduction.* Ottawa: IDRC Books, 1996.

Linton, Marilyn. *Taking Charge by Taking Care: A Canadian Woman's Health Guide.* Toronto: Macmillan, 1996.

McClure, Regan, and Anne Vespry, eds. *Lesbian Health Guide.* Toronto: Queer, 1994.

O'Grady, Kathleen, and Paula Wansborough. *Sweet Secrets: Stories of Menstruation.* Toronto: Second Story Press, 1997.

Rudd, Andrea, and Darlen Taylor, eds. *Positive Women: Voices of Women Living with AIDS.* Toronto: Second Story Press, 1992.

Stoppard, Miriam. *The Breast Book: The Essential Guide to Breast Care and Breast Health for Women of All Ages.* Toronto: Random House, 1996.

Stoppard, Miriam, and Catherine Younger-Lewis. *Canadian Medical Association — A Women's Body: A Manual for Life.* Montreal: Reader's Digest, 1995.

White, Evelyn C., ed. *The Black Women's Health Book: Speaking for Ourselves.* Seattle, WA: Seal Press, 1994.

White, Jocelyn, and Marissa C. Martinez, eds. *Caring for Ourselves: The Lesbian Health Book.* Seattle, WA: Seal Press, 1997.

Zuckweiller, Rebecca. *Living in the Post Mastectomy Body: Learning to Live In and Love Your Body Again.* Vancouver: Hartley and Marks, 1998.

Sexual Harassment

Aggarwal, Arjun P. *Sexual Harassment in the Workplace.* 2nd ed. Markham, ON: Butterworths, 1992.

Bravo, Ellen, and Ellen Cassedy. *The 9 to 5 Guide to Combatting Sexual Harassment: Candid Advice from 9 to 5, the National Association of Working Women.* New York: John Wiley and Sons, Inc. 1992.

Larkin, June. *Sexual Harassment: High School Girls Speak Out.* Toronto: Second Story Press, 1994.

Paludi, Michele A., and Richard B. Barickman. *Sexual Harassment, Work and Education: A Resource Manual for Prevention.* New York: SUNY, 1998.

Spirituality

Allen, Paula G. *The Sacred Hoop: Recovering the Feminine in American Indian Traditions.* Boston: Beacon Press, 1992.

Alpert, Rebecca. *Like Bread on the Seder Plate: Jewish Women and the Transformation of Tradition.* New York: Columbia University Press, 1997.

Baker-Fletcher, Karen. *Sisters of Dust, Sisters of Spirit: Womanist Wording on God and Creation.* Minneapolis: Fortress Press, 1998.

Binet, Noris. *Women on the Inner Journey: Building A Bridge — Healing Racial Wounds through Art and Spirituality.* Nashville, TN: James C. Winston Publishing, 1994.

Christ, Carol P., and Judith Plaskow, eds. *Womanspirit Rising: A Feminist Reader in Religion.* San Francisco: HarperSan Francisco, 1992.

Dyke, Doris Jean. *Crucified Woman.* Toronto: United Church, 1991.

Elder, Jo-Anne, and Colin O'Connell, eds. *Voices and Echoes: Canadian Women's Spirituality.* Waterloo: Wilfrid Laurier University Press, 1997.

Goldstein, Elyse. *Re-Visions: Seeing Torah through a Feminist Lens.* Toronto: Key Porter Books, 1998.

Handley, Shirley. *Nailed to the Church Doors: Conversations with Catholic Women.* Saskatoon, SK: Handley, 1997.

Kyung, Chung Hyun. *Struggle to Be the Sun Again: Introducing Asian Women's Theology.* Maryknoll, NY: ORBIS Books, 1997.

Lebans, Gertrude. *Gathered by the River: Reflections and Essays of Women Doing Ministry.* Toronto: United Church, 1995.

Miller, Christine, and Patricia Chuchryk, eds. *Women of the First Nations: Power, Wisdom, and Strength.* Winnipeg: University of Manitoba Press, 1997.

Monaghan, Patricia. *O Mother Sun! A New View of the Cosmic Feminine.* Freedom, CA: The Crossing Press, 1994.

Native Women's Resource Centre. *Words of Wisdom.* Toronto: Native Women's Resource Centre, n.d.

Sewell, Marilyn, ed. *Cries of the Spirit: A Celebration of Women's Spirituality.* Boston: Beacon Press, 1991.

Vidal, Kim S. *Moon at Her Feet: Images of Women in the Book of Revelation: A Bible Study Guide.* Toronto: United Church, 1998.

Wade-Gayles, Gloria, ed. *My Soul Is A Witness: African-American Women's Spirituality.* Boston: Beacon Press, 1995.

Weisberg, Chana. *Crown of Creation: The Lives of Great Biblical Women Based Upon Rabbinic and Mystical Sources.* Oakville, ON: Mosaic Press, 1996.

Wilson, Lois Miriam. *Telling Her Story: Theology Out of Women's Struggles.* Toronto: United Church, 1992.

Work

Albert, Susan Wittig. *Work of Her Own: A Woman's Guide to Success Off the Career Track.* Los Angeles, CA: Jeremy P. Tarcher, Inc., 1992.

Amato, Sheila, and Pat Staton. *Making Choices: Women in Non-Traditional Jobs.* Toronto: Seacraft, 1991.

Balka, Ellen. *Computer Networking: Spinsters on the Web.* Ottawa: Canadian Research Institute for the Advancement of Women, 1997.

Berg, Astrid. *Finding the Work You Love: A Woman's Career Guide.* San Jose, CA: Resource Publications, Inc. 1994.

Bloomberg, Gerri, and Margaret Holden. *The Women's Job Search Handbook: With Issues and Insights into the Workplace.* Charlotte, VT: Williamson Publishing, 1991.

Dunne, Gillian A. *Lesbian Lifestyles: Women's Work and the Politics of Sexuality.* Toronto: University of Toronto Press, 1996.

Edmiston, Y. Alexandra. *Confessions from the Cubicle: Women Talk About Surviving in Today's Work Force.* Toronto: The Publishing Prose, 1996.

Eyerman, Ann. *Women in the Office: Transitions, Expectations and Possibilities.* Toronto: Second Story Press, Forthcoming 2000.

Finlayson, Judith. *Against the Current: Canadian Women Talk About Fifty Years of Life on the Job.* Toronto: Doubleday, 1995.

Foord Kirk, Janis. *Survivability: Career Strategies for the New World of Work.* Kelowna, BC: Kirkfoord Communications Inc., 1996.

Frank, Tema. *Canada's Best Employers for Women: A Guide for Job Hunters, Employees and Employers.* Toronto: Frank Communications, 1994.

Grandea, Nona. *From Blackboards to Keyboards: The Fragile Link Between Women's Education and Employment.* New York: North-South Books, 1994.

Messing, Karen, Barbara Neis, and Lucie Dumas. *Invisible: Issues in Women's Occupational Health.* Charlottetown, PEI: Gynergy/Ragweed, 1995.

Ontario Women's Directorate and Times Change Employment Service. *Times Change: A Career Planning Workbook for Women.* Toronto: Ontario Women's Directorate, 1994.

______. *A Leader's Guide to Career Planning for Women.* Toronto: Ontario Women's Directorate, 1994.

Parker, Yana. *Resume Pro: The Professional's Guide.* Berkeley, CA: Ten Speed Press, 1993.

______. *The Resume Catalog: 200 Damn Good Examples.* Berkeley, CA: Ten Speed Press, 1996.

Scane, Joyce, Pat Staton, and Margaret Schneider, eds. *Strategies that Work: Women in Trades, Technology and Applied Science.* Toronto: Seacraft, 1994.

Senjen, Rye, and Jane Guthrey. *The Internet for Women.* North Melbourne, AUS: Spinifex, 1996.

Shaw, Eva. *Resumes for Women: Job-Winning Resume Guidance for Every Situation.* New York: Macmillan, 1995.

National Women's Organizations

Women's organizations exist at both the federal and provincial levels. We have listed here a very small selection of national women's organizations. Women's organizations also exist at the municipal level. Please consult your local social services agencies for additional references or consult the municipal / provincial / federal listings in your local telephone book.

Canadian Abortion Rights Action League (CARAL)
1 Nicholas St., Suite 726
Ottawa, ON K1N 7B7
Phone: (613) 789-9956
Fax: (613) 780-9960
E-mail: caral@caral.ca
Web: www.caral.ca/

Canadian Women's Health Network
419 Graham Ave., Suite 203
Winnipeg, MB R3C 0M3
Phone: (204) 942-5500
Fax: (204) 989-2355
E-mail: cwhn@cwhn.ca
Web: www.cwhn.ca

DES Action Canada
(DES Action alerts the public and health professionals to the ongoing dangers of diethylstilbestrol and other synthetic hormones to reproductive health.)

5890 Monkland Ave., Suite 203
Montreal, QB H4A 1G2
Phone: (514) 482-3204
Toll Free: (800) 482-1337
Fax: (514) 482-1445
E-mail: desact@web.net
Web: www.web.net/~desact

Education Wife Assault
427 Bloor Street West
Toronto, ON M5S 1X7
Phone: (416) 968-3422
Fax: (416) 968-2026
E-mail: info@womanabuseprevention.com
Web: www.womanabuseprevention.com

Centres of Excellence in Women's Health (CEWH)
(The Centres exist as partnerships between academics, researchers, health-care providers and community-based women's health organizations. The five centres are listed here.)

Maritime Centre of Excellence for Women's Health
5940 South Street
P.O. Box 3070
Halifax, NS B3J 3G9
Phone: (902) 420-6725
Fax: (902)420-6752
Email: mcewh@dal.ca
Web: www.medicine.dal.ca/mcewh

Centre for Excellence for Women's Health /
Centre D'Excellence pour la Santé des femmes
Université de Montréal Consortium
P.O. Box 6128, Centre-Ville Station
3744 Jean-Brillant, 5th Floor
Montreal, QC H3C 3J7
Phone: (514) 343-6111
Fax: (514) 343-7078
E-mail: cesaf@ere.umontreal.ca
Web: www.cesaf.umontreal.ca/e_home.htm

National Network on Environments and Women's Health
c/o Centre for Health Studies
York University

214 York Lanes
4700 Keele Street
North York, ON M3J 1P3
Phone: (416) 736-5941
Fax: (416) 736-5986
E-mail: nnewh@yorku.ca
Web: www.yorku.ca/research/nnewh/english/nnewhind.html

PRAIRIE WOMEN'S HEALTH CENTRE OF EXCELLENCE
University of Winnipeg
Administrative Centre, 2C11A
515 Portage Avenue
Winnipeg, MB R3B 2E9
Phone: (204) 786-9048
Fax: (204) 774-4134
E-mail: pwhce@uwinnipeg.ca
Web: www.pwhce.ca/

PWHCE REGINA
Phone: (306) 585-5727
Fax: (306) 585-5825
E-mail: pwhce@uregina.ca

PWHCE SASKATOON
Phone: (306) 966-8658
Fax: (306) 966-7920
E-mail: pwhce@usask.ca

BRITISH COLUMBIA CENTRE OF EXCELLENCE FOR WOMEN'S HEALTH
Children's and Women's Hospital
4500 Oak Street, Room E311
Vancouver, BC V6H 3N1
Phone: (604) 875-2633
Fax: (604) 875-3716
E-mail: bccewh@bccewh.ca
Web: www.bccewh.bc.ca/

Federal Government Agencies

Status of Women Canada
360 Albert St., Suite 700
Ottawa, ON K1A 1C3
Phone: (613) 995-7835
Fax: (613) 957-3359
TDD: (613) 996-1322
E-mail: tatzs@swc-cfc.gc.ca
Web: www.swc-cfc.gc.ca/

Women's Health Bureau, Health Canada
0911A Brooke Claxton Bldg.
Tunney's Pasture
Ottawa, ON K1A 0K9
Phone: (613) 957-1945
Fax: (613) 952-3496
E-mail: women's_health_bureau@hc-sc.gc.ca
Web: www.hc-sc.gc.ca/pcb/whb

Sexual Assault, Abuse and Crisis Centres for Women

Crisis centres for women can be found in the yellow pages of the telephone directory for your city under the heading Women's Organizations & Services, or under Social Service Organizations — Sexual Assault Centres.